ON THE READING OF SCRIPTURE

Elijah, the Prophet

D. Peter Burrows, SMA

All rights reserved.
No part of this publication may be reproduced, stored in a retrieval system, or transmitted in any form, or by any means, electronic, mechanical, photocopying, recording or otherwise, without the permission of the author @

peterburrows60@hotmail.com

© Darryl Peter Burrows, March 2015

The right of Darryl Peter Burrows to be identified as
the author of this work has been asserted in accordance with
the Copyright, Designs and Patents Act 1988.

SMA Publications
150 Cours Gambetta
69007 – LYON - FRANCE
sma.mediacenter@gmail.com

Mr. Maclendon, my headmaster for six years of primary school and two years of secondary school was a tough First World War I veteran who taught history as though it was happening in the present, who taught maths so that it made complete sense and who taught Bible as though the world depended on it. For eight years, every schoolday morning we were called to recite: "Study to show thyself approved unto God, a workman that needeth not to be ashamed, rightly dividing the word of truth." Second Timothy 2:15. Mr. Mac made it clear that the Bible was intended for us and for the world, and that it was indeed God's Word of Truth. It was not complicated, but straightforward and comprehensible – and eminently available to me and folks like me.

In the Fifty-five years that I have taught Bible, I have sought to "divide the Word of God's Truth" to make it available – first to myself – and then to others, on the grounds that if God has taken the trouble to make Himself known to humankind, He has certainly not gone out of His way to make that Word complicated, complex or opaque and mysterious. This present work is a part of my continuing attempt to "rightly divide the Word of Truth". I hope that it will help others meet the God who speaks in the Bible on His terms and not on the terms the world would impose on Him.

***

Surely, this commandment that I am commanding you today is not too hard for you, nor is it too far away.

It is not in heaven, that you should say, "Who will go up to heaven for us, and get it for us so that we may hear it and observe it?"

Neither is it beyond the sea, that you should say, "Who will cross to the other side of the sea for us, and get it for us so that we may hear it and observe it?"

No, the word is very near to you; it is in your mouth and in your heart for you to observe.

Deuteronomy 30:11-14 (NRS)

On the Reading of Scripture

Rev. D. Peter Burrows, sma, Ph.D.

How we understand the meaning of any concept in the Bible depends very much upon how we understand the purposes of God as revealed in the text of the Bible and the goals of God concerning the world. If we view the Incarnation of Jesus as the end and purpose of the Old Testament and its narrative and institutions as mere foreshadowings of an entirely new enterprise which begins in Matthew 1.1, we would view the narrative of the Judean monarchy, for example, as a kind of making way for what is to come. What follows the fall of the Kingdom of Judah would be then an inevitable development that the Lord directs to bring about something completely new in keeping with his will. While the last anointed king of Judah does indeed die in Babylon, nonetheless the idea of a messianic king would then undergo a metamorphosis in the intervening years to become suitable as a messianic title for Jesus.

This perception of the Old Testament as a "Sacred History" (German, "Heilsgeschichte") which comes to its fulfilment in the coming of Jesus into the world is the product of German Protestant biblical studies of the mid-nineteenth century until the present. It involved the literary and then the historical-critical study of the Old and New Testament by scholars with a prejudicial bias against Roman Catholicism that was retrojected upon the institutions of ancient Israel. They declared that only the prophetic religion of Israel was authentic and found that the priestly religion of the Pentateuch with its sacrifices, altars, temples, holy days and especially priests were but an exilic and Babylonian invention inserted into the Pentateuchal narrative (and especially the "P" or "Priestly" document), mainly in Leviticus. This judgment on things priestly for these Germans described a bankrupt religion of

Israel that would ultimately give way to the new religion of Jesus, a dying out of the old and rotten to make room for the completely new. Such "scholarship" was subtly anti-Catholic (and anti-Semitic) under the guise of biblical study.

For these commentators and biblical theologians, the only authentic and godly strand of biblical religion was that of the prophets, who shunned tradition and spoke the fresh and direct word of God to the people, a preachment so much like the protestant insistence on the "Word alone". They believed that while some of the prophets went back to the time of the kings and even before, the really authentic prophetic word came from the time of the Babylonian Exile, and much of the prophecies, which were thought to be pre-Exilic, were really only read back into the biblical narrative from the time of the Exile. This they determined by their ingenious (and peculiar, even self-serving) method of historical and literary criticism.

Having dismissed all things priestly and sacrificial in Scripture as being a late development, and seriously impoverished as religion at that, the only institutions left as authentic were the prophets and the Davidic Messiah. However, the messiah for these interpreters was itself an institutional development of the Exile and based upon what they thought to be a future political hope for the restoration of the Kingdom. There was, in this theology, no messianic understanding of the Kings of Judah from David until the Exile. All messianism grew out of a future hope of the restoration of the Kingdom only when it was no more and under foreign domination. In this way, the evil done by the vast number of the Judean kings was dismissed as being of no consequence. They were not really messiahs!

Another feature of this German handling of "history" is the invention of what is called "eschatology", that is, a "study" of the end of days or the last times. The presumption of this eschatology is that the actual religious history of the Old Testament ended with the destruction of the Kingdom of Judah and the Temple in

Jerusalem by the Babylonians, which event gave rise to a yearning for the restoration of all things, but in a new and idealised way. The kingship of Judah that ended in ignominy supposedly became transformed into an idealised "Messianic faith" of the people awaiting fulfilment. This idealisation was, of course, the product of the prophets, most of whose writings came from the time of the Exile. Any sacrificial worship or liturgy that arose during the time of the Exile (and read back into the Pentateuch) was dismissed as empty and formal religion and of no account in God's redemptive plan.

For the Germans, true messianism, then, was an invention of the Exile by the prophets, none of whom actually wrote at the times claimed in the Bible, but only later. They prepared the way for the true idealised Messiah, namely Jesus. The normal and daily experiences of the people of Israel from the destruction of the Temple in 586 BC until the coming of Jesus in 6 BC were really of no account and filled only with a vague "yearning" that God would fix things in due time. Nothing, according to this theory, happened or mattered between Malachi and Matthew. And only those who accepted Jesus as this idealised Messiah (though no one but the Germans 1800 years later seemed to know anything about it) were the real inheritors of the Covenant of God with the people of Israel; the rest were rejected as "the Jews" who had hard hearts and became the enemy of Christianity.[1] The end, in large measure, trivialises the means.

After the resurrection of Jesus from the dead and his ascension into heaven, Christian eschatology then becomes a looking forward to the end of the world when Jesus will come again as the conquering and judging (and fairly unfriendly) heavenly person bringing about the re-gathering of Israel, the rebuilding of the Temple, the resurrection of the Dead and a millennial Sabbath. The more lurid details surrounding all of this were invented by the millennialists[2]

---

[1] It is hard to overlook the latent anti-Semitism in all of this.
[2] Especially the Americans, particularly the Jehovah's Witnesses, the Adventists and the Jewish Christians.

from their reading of the Apocalypse of John, Daniel and selected texts from Ezekiel and elsewhere.

While the German Protestants, and most particularly the virulent anti-Semitic followers of Martin Luther, were not directly responsible for all the later excesses we find today, they nonetheless provided the groundwork. There is no question that Jesus would not recognise the messianism or the eschatology these "scholars" claim to be a development of the later thought of Israel or Judaism. Unfortunately, they do lie behind much of the "Christian" involvement in Israel to this very day. The real problem is the intersection of those who are living in the present times with all of their problems and uncertainties with those who have a florid and imaginary notion of the end of times, and account any present only as preparation for the end. The very peculiar American fundamentalism of today combined with the romantic American doctrines of "Manifest Destiny" has contributed mightily to the mess.

For our purposes, the best proponent of the point of views described above of German Protestant scholarship was the Norwegian scholar, Sigmund Mowinckel in his book, He That Cometh.[3] Of the purpose of the Old Testament, he says:

> The Israelite conception of and belief in kingship are the expression of the desire for some visible human evidence and guarantee of Yahweh's covenant and of His active presence with His people. Yahweh deals with the nation through one of its own members. Israel's own interpretation of her ideal of kingship is given by the author of the Deuteronomic history in his view of history; if the king abides by Yahweh's law, the people will prosper; if the king breaks the law and fails Yahweh, the ruin of the people will follow. *Thus Israel's conception of kingship really points forward to Him who was its true fulfillment.* (Italics mine).[4]

---

[3] Mowinckel, Sigmund, He That Cometh, transl. by G.W. Anderson. Basil Blackwell: Oxford, 1959.
[4] Ibid., p. 95

Of the importance of the Exile to the German School, Mowinckel says:
> The great and decisive line of demarcation in the religious history of Israel and in the development of its religion is the Exile, the destruction of the political life of the nation and the deportation of its spiritual leaders in 598 and 587. Accordingly we speak of the pre-exilic age, the age of the monarchy, the age of the national religion of Israel, and of the post-exilic age, when the monarchy had disappeared and the national state was replaced by the Jewish religious community, which from 520 onwards was gradually consolidated in the province of Judea with Jerusalem at its centre. Besides this Judean, Jewish community in the homeland, a considerable part of the Jewish people continued to live in the Dispersion or Diaspora, the Babylonian Diaspora being the most important and for long the leading one. The spiritual and religious life of Judaism was sustained by the 'Law' and the future hope, the belief that Israel would again be established as an independent nation.[5]

Of the importance of the prophets to Israel's authentic religion, he says:
> The true sources for the Old Testament conceptions of the Messiah are the *prophetic books*; and it is by the tradition-historic and literary criticism of these books that we may discover whether there was any conception of a Messiah in the pre-exilic age.[6]

Of the late dating of those prophetic texts having to do with the Messiah, Mowinckel says:
> It is a fact that the prophetic books consist of collections of prophetic sayings which were handed down over a long period by word of mouth within the circles of these prophets' disciples, until at last they were written down and finally edited. During this process of transmission, there were added sayings which originated within the circle of disciples, and come from later anonymous prophets. It is therefore an assured and inescapable result of criticism that each of the extant prophetic books includes sayings which are later than the prophet with whose

---
[5] Mowinckel, op cit. p. 10. This is the great error of these scholars, namely that they believe the goal of Israel is nationhood and political. This is to misunderstand completely the complexity of intertestamental society.
[6] Ibid., p.15.

name the collection is associated. ... All the other Messianic passages are post-exilic.⁷

In conclusion of this subject, he says:
> A preliminary survey of the sources thus shows that that all the genuinely Messianic passages in the Old Testament date from the time after the fall of the monarchy and the destruction of the Israelite states. ... Anticipating the results of the inquiry in the following chapters, the argument may be stated as follows. 1. The conception of the king in the old royal ideology and in the doctrine (sic!) of the Messiah are in all their main features identical.⁸ 2. The overwhelming majority of the messianic passages belong to the post-exilic age, when the monarchy no longer existed.⁹

Of eschatology and its importance in understanding "Messianic faith", Mowinckel states:
> In later Judaism the term 'Messiah' denotes an *eschatological* figure.¹⁰ He belongs to 'the last time'; his advent lies in the future. To use the word 'Messiah' is to imply eschatology, the last things. It is, therefore, a misuse of the words 'Messiah' and 'Messianic' to apply them, for instance, to those ideas that were associated in Israel or in the ancient east with kings who were actually reigning, even if, as we shall see, these ideas were expressed in exalted and mythical terms. The word 'Messiah' by itself, as a title and a name originated in later Judaism as the designation of an eschatological figure; and it is therefore only to such a figure that it may be applied.¹¹

Of Jesus as the messiah, Mowinckel says:
> In the time of Jesus the Jews were awaiting a Messiah;¹² and it was part of the message of Jesus, and later the central point in

---

⁷ Ibid., pp. 15f. Nowhere does Mowinckel adduce evidence for these claims.
⁸ This "doctrine of the Messiah" is Mowinckel's theological invention and has no basis in fact.
⁹ Ibid., p.20.
¹⁰ Mowinckel makes this assertion without a shred of evidence that it is so!
¹¹ Mowinckel, op. cit., p. 3.
¹² There were no such people as "Jews" in Jesus' day, only "Judeans". Furthermore, Mowinckel does not take any account of the many and diverse "schools" of the "Judaism" in Jesus' time. It is this one assertion, a kind of exegetical sound-bite that has caused the problems concerning the Messiah.

the teaching of His disciples,[13] that He was this Messiah, 'He that cometh'.[14]

We must turn now to a serious flaw in the work of the German exegetes and their disciples before we propose a simpler alternative. The work of the German Protestant biblical interpreters that I have just described arises out of a particular (and somewhat convoluted) philosophy of history developed by Julius Wellhausen (1844-1918) and others for Scriptural studies and is built upon the works of Enlightenment and Rationalist thinkers of the century before. A chief philosopher among them was Georg Hegel. The whole enterprise was built upon a search of independent confirmation of events related in the Bible; this was an attempt to establish "the truth" of Scripture utilising history. While they spoke to the mind and the reason of man, they failed to touch upon the Bible's concern for the plan and purpose of God.

It is abundantly clear that neither history nor the scientific methods have any relationship with the truth of Scripture. Having no real present tense of the verb "to be" makes Scripture completely unsuitable for representations of science and scientific truth, nor in analysing just how God created the heavens and the earth or the like. The Bible was not written as history, and to read it as history or to try to apply some historical method to it is to misunderstand completely the Bible, the people who wrote it and the purpose for which it was written. Historical study of the Bible is defeated by the very language of the Bible, particularly the Hebrew Bible, which has a very different appreciation of time from our modern one. It has only two modalities of action, finished and unfinished; and it is particularly weak in specific definitions of past and future. It is a narrative present which does not lend itself to any sort of historical study or organisation.[15] There is no backwards or

---

[13] Was this really the central point of the disciples' teaching?
[14] Mowinckel, op. cit., p. 3.
[15] Cf. James Barr, Semantics of Biblical Language. Oxford University Press: Oxford, 1961, p. 73, commenting on T Boman, Das hebräische Denken im Vergleich mit dem Griechischen (2nd ed) Göttingen:_____, 1954. James Barr describes T. Boman's analysis of the difference between Hebrew and Greek thinking on time as follows:

forwards in the Bible.[16] Chronological order of event is required for history, and you do not find it in the Bible as a particular

> Boman first connects conceptions of time with verbal systems by saying that "Our idea of time has given itself a plastic expression in our verbs". We (Europeans) think of time as a line; we stand at one point, the present, and the future lies before us and the past behind. Our verbal tense system can be marked off unambiguously by points on this line. There are two mains points combined here: *(a)* time as a line, with future and past lying before and after us *(b)* the tense system of verbs as a marker of points on the line.
>
> In contrast with *(a)* Boman argues that in Hebrew future events are not thought of as lying before us but "always" as coming after us. Neither straight lines nor circles, nor indeed any spatially-related concept, counts for the Hebrew understanding of time. As for *(b)*, in contrast with the European system with its schema of Past, Present and Future, Boman places the Hebrew, which according to him distinguishes two kinds of actions, the complete and the incomplete, because this and not the abstract time reference is what counts when the actions are related to the living rhythm of the person speaking. In other words, the Indo-European verb has a "time" system, and Semitic an "aspect" system, and these are basically different and strange to one another.

I am aware that Dr. Barr has described Boman's thinking here in order to show that it is flawed on philological grounds. Unfortunately, Dr. Barr bases his criticism on his presumption that the Hebrew people were one of history: "How is it possible for a people whose language had no word for "time" and whose verbs were timeless to become the people of *history*, while the Greeks, who had the linguistic apparatus for "time", had a much less powerful apprehension of history?" p. 74. I would maintain that while Dr. Barr may be correct about the Greek, he is certainly incorrect about the Semitic. The Hebrew people are a people of *tradition* (as were probably most of the ancients); but they were not a people of modern, scientific *history*.

Whatever the similarities or differences between classical Greek and Semitic languages, the modern concept of validating truth by establishing the history of an event was in no way the biblical measure for truth and its presentation.

[16] The eleventh century commentator Rashi (Rabbi Solomon ben Isaac) makes the following observation about a discrepancy at the beginning of the Book of Numbers, an observation which becomes normative for the study of the Bible as "history":

> 9. (1) בחדש הראשׁוֹן [AND THE LORD SPAKE UNTO MOSES] IN THE FIRST MONTH – The section which *appears* at the commencement of this Book was not spoken before Eyar (the second month; cf. I. 1): you learn, *therefore*, that there is no "earlier" or "later" (no chronological order) in the Torah - "…בתורה "למדת צאי סדר מקד ומאוטר" " <u>Pentateuch. With Targum Onkelos, Haphtoroth and Rashi's Commentary,</u> "Numbers", Rev. M. Rosenbaum and Dr. A. M. Silberman, transl. and annot. Hebrew Publishing Company: New York, p. 44.)

concern. The same principle must be applied to the study of the New Testament as well. The disparity of chronology within each gospel and among the gospels, and the substantial differences between the synoptic gospels and John, cease to be a problem if we can allow the Bible to be non-historical yet true. However, as parable, the Bible is true at all times, in all places and for all peoples.

Efforts made at the beginning of the last century to analyse the Bible with methods of literary criticism are, in fact, related to the acceptance of history as the measure of the Bible's truth. James Barr observes:

> (there is) a common way of thinking, a common cast of mind and mould of expression, which operates throughout the Bible and which is more noticeable and influential than the variations which it of course undergoes in the minds of individual authors and traditions.
> Two particular circumstances have led to the emphasis on this in the present mid-century theological situation. The first is the reaction against the predominantly analytic and divisive techniques of literary criticism which were so dominant early in the century in biblical study. Against the tendency to fragmentation of the biblical traditions in literary criticism it could now be argued that even where sources were of different origin and interest something of the common biblical mind could be discerned among their variations. Indeed it could be argued that neglect to perceive this common mind and its characteristics was a methodological fault in much literary criticism, and that the divisiveness of these techniques was in part a symptom of the critics' own failure to escape from modern European categories and to perceive the unitary though paradoxical Hebraic mind.[17]

While Barr's particular concern it is not about biblical language, his identification of a "common biblical mind" as being obscured by the literary critic's concern for particular sources (and inevitably, the historical origins and *milieu* of these sources) suggests again that there is a measure for truth that is not historical

---

[17] Barr, op. cit., p. 9.

or historico-critical. In short, literary criticism is a variation of "history equals truth". Samuel Sandmel observes:

> By and large Tanak scholarship has accepted the hypothesis that the Pentateuch is the end result of the blending of J, E, D, and P. We may consider this the usual scholarly conclusion, although there have been dissenters, of course. But the identification of the four sources was only the first step; there still remained the tasks of rooting each of the sources in history, of arranging them chronologically, and of discovering the reasons or purposes that led to their composition.[18]

The connection between literary criticism and the use of history to determine truth is evident here. It is not the identification of literary sources in the five Books of Moses that is the problem with a literary analysis of the truths of the Bible. It is rather the need to determine the dating, the historical impetus for the creation of these sources and their chronological order that leads scholarship to its attempt to verify the truth of the Bible through the means of modern categories of history.

There is, in fact, no problem with the literary analysis that discovers various sources, the Priestly, the Jahvist, the Elohist and the Deuteronomist and their various sub-categories in the Pentateuch. But there is a significant problem created when the insistence on historical dating enters the process. The truth of the Bible, the truth of God's Word, is not verifiable according to the canons of modern history. It is not possible to say that because, from a prejudice about priests, we have dated the "P" source from after the Exile, the "P" source is therefore not really true and valid

---

[18] Samuel Sandmel, The Hebrew Scriptures, 2nd ed. New York: Oxford University Press, 1978, p. 331. Again we note that the "founding fathers" of literary criticism, Julius Wellhausen and his predecessor, K.H. Graf, having proposed a literary strand known as "P", or the Priestly Source, and then dating it after the Exile in Babylon and showing it to be the priestly bankruptcy of Israelite religion, were more convinced of the truth of their theory because they were anti-Roman Catholic Lutherans with a prejudice against all priesthood and its practices than because they were scholars. While they were undoubtedly correct in their isolation of a Priestly source, they were very mistaken in their "historical" presumptions about the lateness and the theological bankruptcy of the "P" source.

about Israel's religion and in the conveyance of God's Word, or worse, it conveys a record of a religion that has lost all vitality and liveliness. "P", "J", "E" and "D" are reasonably discerned in the Pentateuch, but they do exist there *now* as a composite; they are woven together in a text which is a unity and which is, for us as Catholic Christians, true, despite their individual provenance or our prejudices.

We have spoken about history as a modern measure of the truth; the other great system for the measurement of truth in our modern and Western world is, of course, science. For us, if the Bible is to be "true", it must be scientifically true; and if not, we feel intellectually compelled to reduce the Bible to some kind of mythology and then dismiss its truth altogether- for both the Old and the New Testaments alike. Unfortunately, this other system of measurement, science, is not at all the measurement for those who spoke the ancient Hebrew and Aramaic of the Old Testament or who thought and spoke in the Galilean Aramaic of the Gospels (notwithstanding that they were written in a form of ancient Greek).

First of all, Semitic language and the mindset that goes with it are notably deficient in the present tense of the verb "to be". Because it is impossible and not particularly important to ask what a thing or a person is, for these people, scientific truth is really of no importance when talking about God or about the world He has created. Rather, Semitic language, and thus the Bible, will be concerned with what God, people and things *do*, and not what they *are*. Semitic language makes nouns out of verbs, while our own Western languages make verbs out of nouns. Thus a pen and a pencil are identical in Hebrew even though they are made of different materials because they both do the same thing – they write. The Bible is not scientifically true or verifiable simply because God does not reveal His Word in scientific terms or as scientifically verifiable.

It should be evident, then, that any proposed conflict between the story of the creation in the Bible and any of the scientific theories of the origins of the universe is a meaningless and foolish conflict. The Bible does not propose to present an answer to the question, "How (scientifically) did God create the heavens and the earth?" Rather the Word of God in Genesis 1-2 is intended to tell us (in every generation) how the creation is supposed to work and to be maintained (by us) if it is to continue to work according to God's "good" (that is, the way He wants it to work and us to care for it). Darwin's theories are of no concern to the Bible and how we are to maintain the world. We can be biblicists and scientists at the same time – there is no conflict at all – the conflict is wholly imaginary!

Indeed, in more recent times we have come to see that science is itself somewhat uncertain in the establishment of absolute facts and truth. For example, in modern physics the "stuff" called light, which comes from a light bulb, is called a "photon". We know that in the physics we all learned in school, such "stuff" must be either matter or energy; it cannot be both. Yet a photon is matter and it is energy at the same time. It depends on the method we use for measuring it! The same thing is true scientifically for the shortest distance between two points. We know it to be a straight line. Yet in the universe which Einstein showed us, the shortest distance is also a curved line, because the universe is curved. Again, it depends on the measure. Science is at best only relative and is therefore no fit measure for the truth of the Word of God which is not relative nor in any way dependent upon my choice of yardsticks.

The argument that biblical Hebrew's lack of the verb "to be" in the present tense militates against the use of science as a measure of the Bible's truth might find a major objection in Exodus 3:13f, where Moses at the burning bush asks God His name. The reply is usually rendered in our languages as some mysterious form of "BEING" – "I AM THAT I AM" (the King James Version puts it in capitals to emphasise the mystery – as Winnie the Pooh, that wondrous bear of A.A. Milne, lives under the name of

"SAUNDERS"), despite the fact that the word used is probably some futurative form of "is" and certainly not the present tense.

The real point of this story is that God has said to Moses, "I am going to bring My people out of Egypt" and "you, Moses, are going to carry me there." Moses' confusion is evident: "Which 'I' are you talking about?" "I am going to Egypt," says the Lord, "to deliver the people, and you are going to take My I AM there and present Me to Pharaoh." Thus the operative word is the verb "going". "I am GOING and you, Moses, are going to take me there." Perhaps a better translation of the verse would be: "Tell the people that 'I AM GOING TO EGYPT (TO REDEEM YOU)' sent me to you, for my Name is I AM THE ONE THAT IS REALLY GOING – to Pharaoh, to deliver you, to lead you up out of Egypt and to bring you to my land."

A person's name and face are perhaps the closest one can get to talk about someone's "being" in Semitic thought and language, and God's extraordinary concern about not revealing either His name or His face is a serious invitation not to speculate about His Being. And when He finally does reveal his real (and quite a long and fulsome) name to Moses after the giving of the commandments, it is a listing of God's active attributes:
> Know the Lord as one who *acts* with mercy and graciousness, slow to anger and abundant in mercy and truth; Who shows mercy to the multitudes and is patient with regard to iniquity and transgression and sin, yet holds guiltless by no means the wicked; Who visits the iniquity of the fathers upon the children, and upon the children's children to the third and the fourth generation.

"My name is what I do, not who I am."

Again, in the New Testament Gospels, we have Jesus at the Last Supper. He took the bread, said the blessing, broke the bread and gave it to his disciples, saying (presumably in Galilean Aramaic): "This is my body…" Yet he cannot say, "This is"; the word "is" does not appear in his language. And again, he takes the cup, says the blessing and gives it to his disciples, saying (again, in Galilean

Aramaic): "This is my blood...". But he cannot say what there is no word for, and no concept to express it. What is the truth here? The truth is in the verb: "This my body will be broken for you (tomorrow, on the cross); this my blood will be shed for you for the forgiveness of sins (tomorrow, on the cross)." He does not change the bread and wine into anything; rather, he proposes that he will offer the sacrifice of his own body and blood, in which sacrifice we are invited to participate through the breaking of the bread and the taking from the cup. There is no scientific (or in this case, philosophical) conflict here. The truth is in the verb and the verb is "to sacrifice" oneself for sin and its forgiveness.

A collateral issue to be raised at this point is that the Bible and those who wrote it (and the Jewish people today who read it and study it) are neither philosophers nor theologians, at least of the Greek sort. The Greek languages were rich in forms of the verb "to be", and asked such questions as "Who is God?" and "Who am I?" Our theologies continue to explore the existence (by which we mean "being") of God and our own existence and the existence of the world around us borrowing from the richness of Greek concepts of being. Paul Tillich[19], the great German Protestant existentialist theologian described God as the great "Ground of our Being" (*der Boden von unserem Ist sehr*). St. Thomas Aquinas gave us his philosophically and scientifically well-reasoned Summa Theologica. Yet asked why he would not complete the work, he replied: "because all that I have written seems like straw to me." (*Mihi videtur ut palea*).

Yet we continue with the theological sleights (sometimes-even contortions) of hand, in which things remain one thing in appearance while changing their essence through the courtesy of the Greeks in general and Aristotle in particular. But this is not the truth of God's Word, either of Old or New Testament.

---

[19] Tillich, Paul. Systematic Theology: Existence and the Christ (vol. 2). Chicago University Press: Chicago, Ill., Sep. 1973.

Now St. Paul was conversant with Greek philosophies and theologies; yet as a Jew knew them to be flawed, and said so:
> See to it that no one takes you captive through philosophy and empty deceit, according to human tradition, according to the elemental spirits of the universe, and not according to Christ.[20]

This contempt for philosophy is a clear give-away of his struggles of the translation of a mind-set rather than just a linguistic rendition.

God is no great Being to be explored and probed scientifically like a strange and distant galaxy. God is the lead actor on the stage that He created and designed, and He makes Himself presently active for us in His Son, Jesus Christ. "But Jesus answered them, "My Father is still working (on creation), and I also am working."[21] Here he refers to the "work of Creation", the *Ma'aseh Bereshit*. Creation is happening now; "In the beginning…" is now, a present truth and reality, not a fact of the past. We are called to go into that creation to call it back to God, but not to try to "understand" God and His "Being". Jesus called us to believe (trust) in God because of the works that he (Jesus) does.[22]

One other attempt at biblical interpretation to convey the truth of God's Word is to say that the Bible is a myth, or that the God of Israel is a mythological god like the gods of Babylon, Egypt and Canaan. Thus the Bible itself is really mythological and its truth must be seen through the lenses of the myth that it conveys. While the modern mindset would see myth as no more than an instructive "fairy story", there is a real genre of "mythology" in the ancient religions of the world which has to do with the "life" of the gods, their birth, relationships, marriages, sexual qualities and desires. Myth, however, has nothing to do with the truth of the God of Israel and His Word.

---

[20] Col 2:8 (NRS)
[21] Joh 5:17 (NRS). The Rabbis used to say that it was wrong to look behind God's throne, that is, to try to find out who He is and where He came from. It's none of our business, lest we believe we can discover that mystery and become God ourselves – the greatest of all sins.
[22] Joh 10:38

> The basic idea of Israelite religion is that God is supreme over all. There is no realm above or beside him to limit his absolute sovereignty. He is utterly distinct from, and other than, the world; he is subject to no laws, no compulsions, or powers that transcend him. He is, in short, non-mythological. This is the essence of Israelite religion, and that which sets it apart from all forms of paganism. ...The store of biblical legends lacks the fundamental myth of paganism: the theogony. All theogonic motifs are similarly absent. Israel's God has no pedigree, fathers no generations; he neither inherits nor bequeaths his authority. He does not die and is not resurrected. He has no sexual qualities or desires and shows no need of or dependence upon powers outside himself.[23]

All of the above means for determining truth have to do with the truths of our own world – the truths of humankind, which in the final analysis must all be relative. But the truth of God, the truth of the Bible, is different. It transcends the exigencies of our own temporal and spatial experience.

The Holy Father, Benedict XVI, when he was Cardinal Ratzinger, has raised exactly these points in his book, Eschatology, when he states:

> On closer inspection, we can distinguish here two levels whose confusion continually distorts the whole debate. On the one hand, we face a historical problem, an issue of textual interpretation. What does the historian make of the New Testament on this point?[24] What, according to the sources, was the proclamation at that time? What are the most ancient strata that can be traced and how did subsequent development proceed? The historian – in this particular case, the exegete – deals with questions that have to do with the past. He wants to find out exactly "what happened," and so he should. On the other hand, the question as to the meaning of these data from the past for the person who believes, or is searching for faith for today, belongs to quite a different plane. The issue of

---

[23] Yehezkel Kaufmann, The Religion of Israel. The University of Chicago Press: Chicago, Illinois, pp.60f.
[24] The applies equally to the Old Testament.

> appropriation, of the transposition of the past into the present should be carefully distinguished from that of research into historical data. In no way can it be answered by historical methods. It requires quite different methodological tools, corresponding to a different modality of the enquiring spirit. The very supposition that an ancient text has something of value to say to the present and should be interpretively transposed for contemporary digestion already far exceeds the departure point of the historical method. But both sides are guilty of boundary violation. Dogmatics is always tempted to correct the data for the sake of the results. Exegesis wants to perform the task of transposition into the present, claiming the competence of an interpreter for work that simply cannot be carried out in that fashion. Not infrequently, historical analysis suffers from too much touching-up with a view to subsequent reinterpretation.[25]

He says further on:

> Whether or not we think there is truth in the assertion that the Kingdom has come close depends upon what we understand by reality at large: what we consider real and what vantage point within reality we take as our own. Two hundred years ago, the assertion that the Christian hope was illusory would have been completely meaningless for most people in Europe. Though that assertion was in fact made, it remained for most people insubstantial and inconsequential, because the presence of Christianity governed their sense of reality. The Christian message was continually engaged in demonstrating its own reality as something on whose basis one could live and die. The joy which such certitude brought forth, even amidst a host of afflictions, found expression in the radiant beauty of Baroque church-building and music. Today, we are faced with a phenomenon of an absolutely contrary kind.[26]

With regard to science as the means for expressing "the truth", the Holy Father says:

> A second methodological comment is important for evaluating the kind of knowledge which is at stake here. During the last one hundred and fifty years, the epistemological ideal has been that of the natural sciences, where knowledge commends itself as certain

---

[25] Ratzinger, Joseph. Eschatology: Death and Eternal Life, 2nd ed. Catholic University of America Press: Washington, D.C., 1988, pp. 19-20.
[26] Ibid., p. 21.

and useful by techniques of verification and technological application. The historical-critical method tries where possible to transfer this characteristic form which knowledge takes in the natural sciences to the realm of history and to establish as certitude in this sphere that resembles that of the natural sciences themselves. To a remarkable extent this attempt has succeeded in such matters as ascertaining archeological data, deciphering writings, dating documents, recognizing pseudepigraphy, and determining the succession of events. But this method soon discovers its own limitations when called upon to interpret texts with some more weighty significance where such a mode of comprehension is out of the question. The elimination of the observer, never fully possible even in natural science, becomes a mere chimera. And yet people continue to approach the opinions of historical exegetes with a natural scientific model in mind, when the model they should be using is that proper to human history itself.

It is according to this nonhistorical model of the natural sciences that exegetical results are very largely assessed today. They are thought of as a sum of fixed results, a body of knowledge with immaculate credentials, acquired in such a fashion that that it has left behind its own history as a mere history, and is now at our disposal like a set of mathematical measurements. The measuring of the human spirit, however, differs from the quantification of the physical world. To follow the history of exegesis over the last hundred years is to become aware that it reflects the whole spiritual history of that period. Here the observer speaks of the observed only through speaking of himself: the object becomes eloquent only in this indirect refraction. ... Here, too, and especially where the heart of the scriptural message is concerned, there is no such thing as a definitive acquisition of scholarship: no interpretation from the past is ever completely old hat if in its time it turned to the text in true openness. Unfortunately, historical reason's criticism of itself is still in its infancy. But one thing is certain: to employ in this domain the paradigm of knowledge characteristic of the natural sciences is fallacious. Only by listening to the whole history of interpretation can the present be purified by criticism and so brought into a position of genuine encounter with the text concerned.[27]

---

[27] Ibid., pp. 22-24. It would be difficult to overrate this book by the Holy Father in the enterprise of modern, Catholic biblical exegesis and study.

If the Bible is not history, science, ancient literature or archaeological study, we must understand it as something else which conveys God's truth in every time and place and to every person who hears it. Christians accept that Jesus is the Word of God made flesh and dwelling among us; he is comprehensible to us because he is like us in every way except sin. His life, action, preaching and dying are in a world which is the same as our world in the way that it works and the way God reveals Himself in it.

Jesus spoke about the Kingdom of Heaven and about His Heavenly Father; and he promised to continue to do so in the future: "I am with you until the end of the world." The truth of Scripture must be a truth that is always and everywhere true, and true for everyone. And perhaps the useful word for naming this truth of God's Word is "parable". "Parable" expresses truth that is in keeping with the Bible's emphasis on action in the verb. While it is not myth, it does permit of an expression of truth that is not restricted by specific time or place. Jesus uses parable in his own teaching for this very reason.

The Greek παραβολή is used in the Greek Bible to translate the Hebrew מָשָׁל (_mashal_). It means "juxtaposition", that is: this situation is like that situation. But it is different from an allegory in that the comparison (the "likeness") is between two action-situations rather than between two things or people. Thus the action or operation of the Kingdom of Heaven is like what happens in our situation when … . The name of the Prodigal Son is not important; his name is my name. What he does in the parable is what I do from time to time in my own life. The Father's behaviour towards his prodigal son is the way God acts towards me – with mercy rather than justice. And I am the older brother, the jealous one, as well – and just like Cain in the Book of Genesis. It is small wonder that the parables of Jesus enraged so many – he was telling them about themselves in God-speak and they did not like it. Small wonder, too, that some of the Pharisees of Jesus' times so disliked his teaching in parables: the shoe fit too snugly. They knew exactly whom the parables were about – they recognised their own behaviour. And I, two thousand years later and miles away from Israel, can still know the truth of what God's Word is for me.

This is not to suggest that the Bible was written for devotional purposes or to inspire individual faith. Nor is to be dismissed as a mythological or symbolic collection of prose and poetry for purposes of entertainment. While it is truth that cannot be proven, it is not intended for the gullible or weak-minded either, as faith is so often (improperly) defined. Rather, the Bible is a clear and robust declaration in the language and form of parable of the affirmation that there is a single God who created everything as a place for Himself and how this affirmation works out in human experience, including my own.

Just as parable is a timeless and placeless way of describing reality according to the timeless actions and dynamics of that reality, so in biblical terms, liturgy and liturgical repetitions are simply one form of parable. In Scripture, regular recitation of an event creates the reality of that event in any present time and place.[28] Recollection is reality. This is a difficult concept for the modern scientific and historical mind.

I propose to give here some fundamental assertions about the intent of the Bible that will, I hope, provide a context for a modern reading of Scripture. These assertions are, I believe, in accord with what James Barr has identified above as "a common way of thinking, a common cast of mind and mould of expression, which operates throughout the Bible," and what Pope Benedict has called "a different modality of the enquiring spirit" for the appropriation, of the transposition of the past into the present.

---

[28] In the Catholic Mass, this recollection, which creates present reality, is called *anamnesis* (ἀνάμνησις). In Judaism, the recitation of the Passover Haggadah creates the reality of the Exodus and subsequent events in the present; thus there are no verbs in the past tense used in the narrative.

THE ASSERTIONS

Assertion 1: The mind-set of the world of the Bible is concerned with purpose and with planning for purpose; it is <u>not</u> concerned with meaning. Biblical language, especially the Semitic languages, are based upon verbs rather than nouns and thus upon action rather than reflection. Even the Greek of the New Testament, especially the Greek of St. Paul, testifies to a struggle to translate the Semitic mind-set into contemporary (rather than Classical) Greek. The somewhat contorted writings of St. Paul become much easier when his purpose of bringing the Bible to the Greeks is born in mind.

The search for meaning, while sympathetic to modern science, philosophy, theology, spirituality and reflection upon the world or life in general, is foreign to the Bible. The general tendency of the concern for the discovery of meaning is towards inertia – a thinking about being that goes nowhere and makes no plans for the journey. The ancient Christian heresy of Gnosticism in all its forms arises from a concern for meaning arising from the Greek mind-set.

The concern for meaning is attractive because it is fairly risk-free. While it can create worlds from the spider-webs of thoughts, these worlds can be discarded as quickly as they can be created and no responsibility need be taken for anything. Further, the assignment of and reflection upon meaning are highly subjective and relative to my own state of mind. Reading Scripture to find meaning for life and the world lead to excesses of the ego that miss completely the purpose of Holy Scripture. A spirituality based upon meaning can very soon become selfish and self-indulgent.

If, when reading or studying the Bible, we can set aside our modern search for meaning and turn to the original mind-set, which saw the Scriptures as a declaration of purpose and a plan for achieving that purpose, we are more likely to enter that dialogue with deity which the Scriptures invite.

By speaking of planning for purpose, I am not suggesting that the Bible is an ethical handbook and list of laws whose fulfilment guarantees heaven. This was rejected by Jesus in the parable of the rich young man who asks for the plan for eternal life. When Jesus suggests a righteous life, the man turns this into his pride that he has kept commandments all his life. Jesus, aware that the man's plan is based upon the wrong purpose, that is, achievement of eternal life for himself, gives a suggestion that will return the man to the real purpose of God – to redeem the world. "Go and divest yourself of your own riches (and your hopes to keep your riches after you die) and come, follow me (in God's work of preaching repentance and redeeming the world)." The poor rich man cannot move from the meaning he has given to life with his riches to the purpose of God for the world.[29] The Law cannot save; but even more important, my *personal* salvation is not even the issue in the purpose of God!

The parable of Mary and Martha might suggest the importance of reflecting upon meaning, but this is to miss the import of this narrative. The question providing the context of the parable is: What are the laws which assure doing the Good? The answer, of course, is to be found in those laws of the love of God and the love of neighbour (which is extended to the love of one's fellow human being). The second implicit question is: Of the two laws, which is the very first? The answer is the parable. Martha shows the fulfilment of the law concerning one's fellow, that is, by showing hospitality. Mary, however, is fixed on the first law which is primary commitment to the Lord, and hers is the best; for without prior commitment to God, even the second is fruitless. Here Mary is not searching for meaning nor is she meditating on the teaching of Jesus; she is making a simple choice, and it is her choice of the Lord even over extending hospitality that is significant.[30]

---

[29] Luk 18.18-25
[30] Luk 10.38-42

Assertion 2: The God of the Bible is a particular God with identity and purpose. The God who speaks in the Bible is not an abstract notion of deity nor is he divine principle or idea.[31] He is not the end result of human reasoning, nor is he any kind of summary of human conclusions about gods or powers. The God of the Bible did not emerge from a prior polytheistic era in Israel's (or anyone else's) history. As creator of humanity, he is before humanity and quite apart from humanity. He is not created in the image of humanity nor is he an answer to some human need or yearning. He cannot be discovered by reason or intellectual exercise; he is either accepted or not.

God's particularity is indicated by his name, which in Semitic fashion is a name of action rather than being. A person's name and face are perhaps the closest one can get to talk about someone's "being" in Semitic thought and language, and God's extraordinary concern about not revealing either His name or His face is a serious invitation *not* to speculate about His Being. When He finally does reveal his real (and quite a long and fulsome) name to Moses after the giving of the commandments, it is a listing of God's *active* attributes:
> Know the Lord as one who ACTS with mercy and graciousness, slow to anger and abundant in mercy and truth; Who shows mercy to the multitudes and is patient with regard to iniquity and transgression and sin, yet holds guiltless by no means the wicked; Who visits the iniquity of the fathers upon the children, and upon the children's children to the third and the fourth generation.[32]

His name is what he does, not who he is. This name is revealed and not reasoned. It is not the object of or for human reflection; it simply identifies him by his actions. Thus, when we see mercy occurring in the world or behold justice at work, we know of the involvement of the God of the Bible.

---

[31] The God of the American motto, "In God We Trust", is unfortunately such an abstraction.
[32] Exodus 34:6f (my transl.) And even here, the Lord refuses to show His face. See also Jonah 4:2.

Just as God's identity is revealed in Scripture, so also is his purpose in his creation. His purpose precedes the creation of humankind and is quite separate and prior to any purposes or plans of humankind. The attribution of human will or human purpose to God is folly, on the principle of: "For my thoughts are not your thoughts, nor are your ways my ways, says the LORD."[33]

Assertion 3: The first verse of Genesis, "In the beginning, God created the heavens and the earth," sets forth four primary concepts that undergird all the rest of the biblical narrative. These four concepts are: the priority and uniqueness of God; the knowledge of God through His actions; the difference between God and that which He creates ("the heavens and the earth"); and the principle assumption that God is always subjective and everything else, including humanity, is objective.

The Priority and Uniqueness of God: There is no biblical narrative to prepare us for the act of creation. We are not told about any preliminaries, any developments, any non-personal happenings or any other events that would prepare us to expect the creation of the heavens and the earth. God's "Existence" before creation is never explored (especially since there is no Hebrew word for "exist").[34] We cannot discern anything about motive from this first verse. The only part of the verse that is familiar if we had no other verses is that which we ourselves experience – "the heavens and the earth." God, and no one nor anything else confronts us here, just as He confronts others like Abraham and Moses later on in the narrative - that is, unexpectedly and alone and from totally elsewhere. We cannot imagine or infer him from our place in "the heavens and the earth."[35] God comes to our experience from outside it. God is a surprise!

---

[33] Isa 55:8 (NRS)
[34] The answer to the child's inevitable question when hearing the parable of creation, "Where did God come from?" can only be answered, "He didn't come from anywhere."
[35] Even St. Paul in Romans 1:20 allows that the pagans should have been able to infer the everlasting power and deity of God in their mind's eye, but only *"ever since* God created the world", but certainly not before.

The Knowledge of God through His Actions: As we have noted earlier concerning parable, the Bible runs immediately to the verb – to the action and movement. We might say that the Bible is dynamic rather than essential and static. Our first verse in Hebrew has the verb in second place following the opening (rather mysterious) adverb "in the beginning" (בְּרֵאשִׁית). The verb, *ba'ra* (בָּרָא), is used only with God as its subject and with the meaning, "to shape, fashion or create". The object of the verb can be "the heavens and the earth", "humankind", "individual humans", "new conditions or circumstances" and "transformations" (i.e., new hearts or new heavens and earth). This verb is a kind of parable in itself, for as it is used to describe divine activity only, it invites the question: "To what may it be compared in our own experience?" The answer is: "When God creates, it is like the human action of "making or fashioning" something[36] from within the heavens and the earth.

This dynamism of God and the continuing of creation are signed in the vision of Isaiah of God in the Temple: "Above him stood the seraphim; each had six wings: with two he covered his face, and with two he covered his feet, and with two he flew."[37] The wings cover those points on the divine person, which are the points of power. The face or visage is the place of the name of God, his identity and majesty upon which he wears the crown. The feet represent the reproductive organs where life is created and creativity occurs. The place of flight is the dynamic of the Almighty, constantly in purposive action and always at "work" in the creation. There is no stasis about the living God of Israel, and each of these power points is defined as "holy".

A corollary of this assertion is that the mindset of Scripture has little concern for cause and effect when speaking of God. In fact, it pays little mind to the principle when dealing with God's creativity either. This has to do again with the weakness of the

---

[36] The wonderful pun concerning Jesus' father is that he is the son of a carpenter (a "maker" of things) and the Son of God (the "creator" of all things).
[37] Isa 6:2 (RSV)

verb "to be" in the present tense in biblical Hebrew and the presumption that any cause in the created world cannot take account of the hidden and unexpectable involvement of God in all events concerning his creation.

For example, we are told that Abraham and his wife Sarah are barren:
> Then Abraham fell on his face and laughed, and said to himself, "Can a child be born to a man who is a hundred years old? Can Sarah, who is ninety years old, bear a child?"[38]
> Now Abraham and Sarah were old, advanced in age; it had ceased to be with Sarah after the manner of women. So Sarah laughed to herself, saying, "After I have grown old, and my husband is old, shall I have pleasure?" The LORD said to Abraham, "Why did Sarah laugh, and say, 'Shall I indeed bear a child, now that I am old?' Is anything too wonderful for the LORD? At the set time I will return to you, in due season, and Sarah shall have a son." But Sarah denied, saying, "I did not laugh"; for she was afraid. He said, "Oh yes, you did laugh."[39]
> The LORD dealt with Sarah as he had said, and the LORD did for Sarah as he had promised. Sarah conceived and bore Abraham a son in his old age, at the time of which God had spoken to him. Abraham gave the name Isaac to his son whom Sarah bore him.[40]

Sarah laughs because in the normal way of the world, cause says that her bareness must lead to the effect that God's promise for a child will be of no effect. That Isaac is born is an exception from cause and effect because of God's intervention due to God's purposes. Abraham's faith in this God involves something more than simple cause and effect, as it says:
> Now faith is the assurance of things hoped for, the conviction of things not seen. Indeed, by faith our ancestors received approval. By faith we understand that the worlds were prepared by the

---

[38] Gen 17:17 (NRS)
[39] Gen 18:11-15 (NRS)
[40] Gen 21:1-3 (NRS)

word of God, so that what is seen was made from things that are not visible.⁴¹

Biblical Hebrew does have a stem of the verb called the "Hiphil" which is sometimes described as "causative". Thus, the Qal Stem of the verb זָכַר (he remembered) becomes in the Hiphil Stem הִזְכִּיר (he caused to remember/he reminded), this has little to do with the philosophical and modern scientific notion of causality. As we have seen, God did not "cause the creation" (the Hiphil of the present tense of "to be" – which does not exist!). Rather, God <u>created</u> the heavens and earth at his pleasure, and we cannot reason back from the effect to the cause. Science is wonderful but it cannot take account of the Creator lurking behind the creation with his own purposes in mind. This the world cannot comprehend. The closest that modern science can come to this notion is when modern physics speaks of the randomness in quantum theory.

It is for the same reasons that cause and effect are alien to the Bible that we do not find anything corresponding to coincidence in the Bible either. We have pointed out in Assertion 1 that the Bible is concerned with purpose and not meaning. "Coincidence is a way of giving meaning to a collection of two or more events or conditions, closely related by time, space, form, or other associations which appear unlikely to bear a relationship as either cause to effect or effects of a shared cause, within the observer's or observers' understanding of what cause can produce what effects."⁴² Because the Bible is primarily concerned with God and his purpose for the creation, it will always look for God's purpose rather than to accident to explain events. Again, modern physics and quantum mechanics and the appeal to "randomness" as a lack of pattern or predictability in events would never arise in the minds of those who received the Scriptures.⁴³

---

⁴¹ Heb 11:1-3 (NRS)
⁴² "Coincidence", from Wikipedia, the Free Encyclopedia.
⁴³ And Erwin Schrödinger's cat would never have had a problem!

The Difference between God and That Which He Creates: This "difference" is implicit in the very first word of our verse: "In the beginning" (*b'reshith* –בְּרֵאשִׁית). This is a mysterious adverb in that when it is used about God's creation, it has neither the meaning of time ("in the beginning of time") nor place ("at this starting point or place") which it would suggest if it were used about us and our making or fashioning something. The first letter, *beth* (בְּ), is here not static, as in "in" or "at". It has a sense of movement in it, such as "from" or "in the milieu of". We might even translate the word as a parable: "Way back there when the world was just beginning", or some such thing.

The reason for the obscurity of the word is to affirm that God does not come from "some*where*" or "some*time*", nor does He begin His creation at a specific time or place. This is further affirmed by the later narrative that God creates "place" on the third day of the week and "time" on the fourth day with the sun, moon and stars by which we are to tell time. "In the beginning...", then, means before the creation of time on the fourth day of the week and before the creation of place on the third day of the week. And because God stands outside of time and place, His creative Word then falls on all points in creation at all times.

The simple yet most profound affirmation of this wonderful word at the very head of the Bible is that there is a radical difference between God's perspective and ours. God's actions, unlike ours, are not confined by anything, like time and place, which He goes on to create, for His "doings" are beginning before the beginning (of time and place). Thus, from our human standpoint, God is always creating – even in my time and place. So Jesus can say, "The Kingdom of Heaven is very near you,"[44] and John can declare, "The Word becomes flesh and dwells among us."[45]

The Assumption that God Is Always Subjective and Everything Else Is Objective, including Humanity: The Hebrew language has

---

[44] Lk 10.9
[45] Jn 1.14

a specific word for identifying the object of a verb and thus distinguishing subject from object. The word, a particle really, is *"'eth"* (אֵת). It is composed of the first and last letter of the Hebrew alphabet, which may or may not be significant in indicating the distance between God and His world. It is used in our first verse attached to both "the heavens" and "the earth". This tiny bit of a word defines the relationship between God and creation (and most especially humankind) throughout all of Scripture, and the religion that derives from it. It says, "God is completely prior to and apart from His creation; that He owns it because He made it; and He cannot be represented by any part of it."

Thus we have, in the very first verse, the principle which later will be articulated in all the commandments against idolatry, graven images and the inclination of the powerful to declare themselves "god". God is always the Subject; we and our world are always the object. All things and people in the creation are wholly derivative and dependent. To wonder about the origins of God is like wondering about who invented the starting block when the race is well underway.

It is clear, then, that anyone without a willingness to at least entertain a God of specific and unique identity who is prior to humanity and with a purpose quite apart from human purpose should probably not undertake to read the Bible at all, for without the reader's willingness to accept these presumptions, the Bible will not make any particular sense.

Assertion 4: God created the heavens and the earth, that is, the universe or "everything", for himself. When it says at each stage of creation that God says, "It is good," we are meant to know that it is good *for God* – it is fit for his purpose. It would be human arrogance to assume from the text that God created the vast expanse of the universe for human beings. Furthermore, human beings do not even enter the narrative until the second chapter of

Genesis and are portrayed there as hardly the motive for creation at all.

The association of creation with the later temples and the tabernacle of Israel indicate the Bible's understanding that God made the creation for himself as a dwelling place, a habitation or temple/palace for himself. The image of the king having a palace surrounded by a garden is the one operative here and throughout the Scriptures. He made it for himself because he is the king, and there should be no mistake about ownership, for:
> The earth is the LORD's and all that is in it, the world, and those who live in it; for he has founded it on the seas, and established it on the rivers.[46]

And again,
> So acknowledge today and take to heart that the LORD is God in heaven above and on the earth beneath; there is no other.[47]
> Although heaven and the heaven of heavens belong to the LORD your God, the earth with all that is in it, yet the LORD set his heart in love on your ancestors alone and chose you, their descendants after them, out of all the peoples, as it is today.[48]

It is holy because the Holy One lives in it. The final act of creation is the act of God's moving into his place or taking his rest in his own abode. This is the significance of the Sabbath Day – the day he took occupancy. Of that day, Scripture says: "But the LORD is in his holy temple; let all the earth keep silence before him!"[49]

For those who believe that God created the world for them rather than himself, they have only to read the parable of Jesus in Mark 12 concerning those who believe that the vineyard was theirs to receive clarification on this fundamental principle of Scripture.

Environmentalists will take hope from this assertion concerning creation and its purpose.

---

[46] Psa 24:1-2 (NRS)
[47] Deu 4:39 (NRS)
[48] Deu 10:14-15 (NRS)
[49] Hab 2:20-1 (NRS)

Assertion 5: In the parable of creation there is no suggestion of how God created the heavens and the earth. Rather we are given the four general principles by which the universe operates. Before God speaks, the universe is a formless void (no boundaries); a great and swirling darkness sits upon it (no recognition); and the mighty wind rushes aimlessly over the waters (no direction or goals). This chaos is the biblical concept of hell, and the Bible often describes it as a mighty storm. When the Word of God which holds up the world is rejected or neglected, "all hell breaks loose" and causes great fear to those who are caught in it. This fear is, at its root, the fear of death, or being "scared to death". The antidote to hell and fear is the Word of God which brings order to the chaos. Keeping the Word of God is called "righteousness" and rolls back the storm, the flood, and hell.

God speaks to the chaos and says, "Light!" Light appears, and immediately God divides the light from the darkness, creating a boundary that brings order to the chaos. Then he names the light day and the darkness night. By giving names to the two parts God exercises dominion over them and gives them each a separate identity and value, thus bringing further order into the chaos. Finally God imposes a balance between the two[50]. This balance when maintained between two human beings is the Bible's meaning of "love". Of these principles in operation God says of them, "This is "the good." It should be noted that "the good" has no moral implications here; it is simply the universe working as it is supposed to do. Boundaries, the value of the parts and the balance between them define "the good". A fourth universal principle is given on the fifth and sixth days of creation when God creates the fish, birds and land animals with the insects. His blessing on them, "Be fruitful, increase and overrun the earth" establishes that *life is the prime directive of the universe.* To live according to these principles is to do "the good", maintaining righteousness and keeping hell at bay.

---

[50] See especially "and light shines in darkness, and darkness could not overpower it." Joh 1:5 (NJB)

These universal principles pertaining to the "good" of creation, then, are:
1. Boundaries and separations (the fundamental order of things)
2. Names and identifications (which are the Bible's "reality")
3. Balance and relationships (including "love" between humans)
4. The priority of life[51]

We must note that these principles are God-established and given, are established before the creation of Adam, and are in no way subject to human validation or manipulation. They are unchanging, and while humans are given free will later which can support (doing the good) or defy (doing the evil), human beings can in no way change them – they are built into the creation itself.

When the Bible speaks of the Torah, "instructions", it is to these four principles that it refers. These are the instructions for maintaining the order of the universe and according to which the creation is to operate. These are not "laws"; they simply tell us humans how to keep the world from falling down. To ignore them is what the Bible calls "folly".

Assertion 6: While the Bible knows nothing of modern science and its categories, it very often uses a vocabulary which is familiar to us moderns while not investing words with the same values that we have for them. The failure to appreciate the differences often leads to serious misunderstandings of Scripture. Perhaps the most seriously misunderstood word, even more than "love" (though "love" is a very close second) are the words "to live" and "to breathe" used together- that is, having "living breath" (the "breath of life) or "animating breath" (נֶפֶשׁ חַיָּה) in it.[52] As pointed out above, life is the fourth universal principle of creation itself and is therefore a given of creation. It has no opposite ("death" is not, for the Bible, the opposite of "life") and God had nothing to do with death's creation or appearance. Nor is death God's punishment for sin.

---

[51] For a confirmation of these principles in Scripture, see Sirach (Ecclesiasticus) 42:15-25.
[52] This is sometimes incorrectly translated as "soul" with all of the attendant Christian philosophical baggage loaded on this word. Hebrew is simpler – if it breathes, it is alive and a living "critter".

After the flood in the days of Noah, God makes a covenant between himself and all that pertains to life in creation: "the everlasting covenant between God and every living creature of all flesh that is upon the earth." בֵּין אֱלֹהִים וּבֵין כָּל־נֶפֶשׁ חַיָּה בְּכָל־בָּשָׂר אֲשֶׁר עַל־הָאָרֶץ:[53]

It is this unitary sense of the wholeness of life in creation that is intended by the fourth universal principle of creation. God makes a covenant between himself and life itself in its totality following the flood. We moderns have agreed that life belongs to individual manifestations of it, an individual dog, bird, fish, human being which is, as we say, a living "being". The Bible, even when it speaks of individuals, presumes the wholeness of life which precedes any individual manifestation of it. The life is, fundamentally, a creation of God, belongs to God, and persists at his pleasure, the product of his word: "Let there be life!"

That life is to be fulsome in creation, both in the spatial and the temporal dimensions of that creation is expressed by the blessing which God gives to life: "God blessed them, saying, 'Be fruitful and multiply and fill the waters in the seas, and let birds multiply on the earth,'"[54] וַיְבָרֶךְ אֹתָם אֱלֹהִים לֵאמֹר פְּרוּ וּרְבוּ וּמִלְאוּ אֶת־הַמַּיִם בַּיַּמִּים וְהָעוֹף יִרֶב בָּאָרֶץ: A blessing in the Bible indicates the lifting of a restriction or an opening of that which was shut. Thus the blessing itself suggests the outpouring of life in creation without limit. The command to "be fruitful and multiply" is in fact the order to fill time with life, from one generation to another in perpetuity and without limit. The commands to "fill" and to "multiply" are spatial – let everywhere teem with life. Unlimited and perpetual life is a primary function of creation itself! Life is pervasive, and that is the way God wants it.

As in our own science, human beings are themselves a part of living things (we would say "animals"); they are a part of the continuum of life and blessed with the blessing:

---

[53] Gen 9:16 (JPS)
[54] Gen 1:22 (NRS)

> God blessed them, and God said to them, "Be fruitful and multiply, and fill the earth and subdue it; and have dominion over the fish of the sea and over the birds of the air and over every living thing that moves upon the earth."[55]

The difference in this passage between humans and the other animals is that humans are given the right to "rule over" or "subjugate" (רדה) all the other animals. Clearly, this capacity to "rule" is the direct consequence of being created in the "image and likeness of God" and implies here a control over the life itself of the other animals, a significant power. Later, after the Flood, the power is extended to being permitted to "take the life" of animals in the sense of slaughter for meat and for sacrifice. This is described as the "dread fear" which the animals have for humans:

> God blessed Noah and his sons, and said to them, "Be fruitful and multiply, and fill the earth. The fear and dread of you shall rest on every animal of the earth, and on every bird of the air, on everything that creeps on the ground, and on all the fish of the sea; into your hand they are delivered. Every moving thing that lives shall be food for you; and just as I gave you the green plants, I [now] give you everything.[56]

Before the flood and the granting of this permission to take life, any taking of life, even slaughter, was classed as "murder", that is, the taking of life without the permission of the life-giver. And even when humankind is given permission to take animal life for food and sacrifice, nonetheless humans may not take each other's lives:

> For your own lifeblood I will surely require a reckoning: from every animal I will require it and from human beings, each one for the blood of another, I will require a reckoning for human life. Whoever sheds the blood of a human, by a human shall that person's blood be shed; for in his own image God made humankind.[57]

---

[55] Gen 1:28 (NRS)
[56] Gen 9:1-3 (NRS)
[57] Gen 9:5-6 (NRS)

Assertion 7: The purpose of human beings[58] in creation is clearly stated at the beginning: "Yahweh God took the man and settled him in the garden of Eden to cultivate and take care of it."[59] The verb "to cultivate" is, in Hebrew, "to serve" (עָבַד). The objection to translating the verb as "cultivate" was raised by ancient commentators, who pointed out that it needed no cultivation on the grounds that:

> Out of the ground the LORD God made to grow every tree that is pleasant to the sight and good for food, the tree of life also in the midst of the garden, and the tree of the knowledge of good and evil. A river flows out of Eden to water the garden, and from there it divides and becomes four branches.[60]

The second verb, "to care for" (שָׁמַר), can mean "be careful about" or "protect" and also "to guard" or "to watch". The name of the Samaritans is thought to come from this root, meaning the guardians of the Law of God. Perhaps an ancient translation, though a marginal one of the Samaritans, of this verse is: "God placed humankind in the garden to serve Him by watching over it."

God's purpose in creating humankind, then, is to care for his dwelling place. Creation is not given to Adam but entrusted to humankind for safekeeping. Humans do not own creation; they are established in it as the gardeners and caretakers. Moreover, they have been given the instructions for its maintenance – "the Good".

Assertion 8: Because of the radical and absolute discontinuity between God and any part of his creation, God is unknowable to creation except to humankind, and this is because God created humankind in his own image and likeness:

> Then God said, "Let us make humankind in our image, according to our likeness; and let them have dominion over the fish of the sea, and over the birds of the air, and over the cattle, and over all the wild animals of the earth, and over every creeping thing that creeps upon the earth." So God created humankind in his image,

---

[58] The Hebrew word *adam* (הָאָדָם) means "humankind" or "human beings", not "man". Note again that humans in the Bible do not have "natures." They have purpose.
[59] Gen 2:15 (NJB)
[60] Gen 2:9-10 (NRS)

in the image of God he created them; male and female he created them.[61]

Even to humankind God is not known; rather he may be inferred from the image of God which he bears. We humans are, in fact, a parable of God, and the inference may be gently reversed – though not perfectly in that "My ways are not your ways" in the end. St. Paul, in his letter to the Romans, makes this point:

> For what can be known about God is plain to them, because God has shown it to them. Ever since the creation of the world his eternal power and divine nature, invisible though they are, have been understood and seen through the things he has made. So they are without excuse; for though they knew God, they did not honor him as God or give thanks to him, but they became futile in their thinking, and their senseless minds were darkened.[62]

Thus, theology is foreign to Scripture, if by theology we mean a claim to know God. We may say, "We infer that God has free will since we enjoy that power and we are made in his image and likeness." We may further infer that the animals do not have free will and thus we are superior to them in our likeness to the Creator. However, we may never say that God is created in the image and likeness of man. In short, we hold that God knows us by having created us; but we do not know God and may only infer him.

There is a corollary of this assertion. While humankind cannot know God by its own efforts, God can make his purpose (not his "being") known to select and designated humans by his spirit, called the "Holy Spirit", which can move from the incorporeal God to the incorporeal mind of man. Those who receive such instructions are designated (and usually signed in some way) by God. Thus we have the simple statement, "Now the LORD said to Abram,..."[63], not in what we think of as talking, but by means of God's Spirit communicating his purposes to Abraham. The Bible would consider Abraham's talking back as prayer. That prayer need not be oral as is shown in the wonderful story of Hannah's inarticulate prayer in the tabernacle at Shiloh as she prays for a

---

[61] Gen 1:26-27 (NRS)
[62] Rom 1:19-21 (NRS)
[63] Gen 12:1 (NRS)

son: "Hannah was praying silently; only her lips moved, but her voice was not heard; therefore Eli thought she was drunk."[64] God does not answer Hannah directly, but shares his purpose through his designated agent, the old priest-prophet Eli.

The prophets are those who are the designated agents most often of God's shared plans. This is especially true from the time of Moses, about whom God says:
> Now the man Moses was very humble, more so than anyone else on the face of the earth. ... And he (the Lord) said, "Hear my words: When there are prophets among you, I the LORD make myself known to them in visions; I speak to them in dreams.
> Not so with my servant Moses; he is entrusted with all my house. With him I speak face to face-- clearly, not in riddles; and he beholds the form of the LORD.[65]

That all are not prophets is indicated by Moses' expostulation:
> But Moses said to him, "Are you jealous for my sake? Would that all the LORD's people were prophets, and that the LORD would put his spirit on them!"[66]

That the prophet is of God's choosing and not through human designation is stated:
> Two men remained in the camp, one named Eldad, and the other named Medad, and the spirit rested on them; they were among those registered, but they had not gone out to the tent, and so they prophesied in the camp. And a young man ran and told Moses, "Eldad and Medad are prophesying in the camp." And Joshua son of Nun, the assistant of Moses, one of his chosen men, said, "My lord Moses, stop them!"[67]

Solomon's prayer at the dedication of the Temple is for wisdom - that is, to know how to govern God's people according to God's plan and will - suggests that anointed kings of God's people have the prophetic designation in matters of governance.[68] This

---

[64] 1Sa 1:13 (NRS)
[65] Num 12:3, 6-8 (NRS)
[66] Num 11:29 (NRS)
[67] Num 11:26-28 (NRS). For a broader discussion on prophecy in Israel, see the section below on Israel's institutions in the wilderness.
[68] I Ki 3:9

prophetic role of the kings is first described at the designation of Saul as king of Israel, where Saul is anointed with oil and found immediately to be part of a band of prophets.[69]

The sign of oil used to anoint the speaker as God's agent for his Holy Spirit is to be found first (formally) in the anointing of Aaron as High Priest by Moses at God's behest.[70] The rather strange and contorted relationship of God, Moses and Aaron at the burning bush is also suggestive of the prophetic communication between God and the people:

> But he said, "O my Lord, please send someone else." Then the anger of the LORD was kindled against Moses and he said, "What of your brother Aaron, the Levite? I know that he can speak fluently; even now he is coming out to meet you, and when he sees you his heart will be glad. You shall speak to him and put the words in his mouth; and I will be with your mouth and with his mouth, and will teach you what you shall do. He indeed shall speak for you to the people; he shall serve as a mouth for you, and you shall serve as God for him.[71]

All of this has to do with conveying the mind of God to his people.

Assertion 9: This follows from the previous assertion. While the Bible recognizes that some peoples and nations have gods that they worship, at the same time the Bible maintains that such gods are meaningless and have no reality. When God first created Adam, he recognized that if Adam was in God's own image and likeness and he was alone as God is alone, Adam might get the idea that he is god. Thus, God said: "It is not good that Adam should be alone; I will make another one of them."[72] By creating humankind plural and social, God seeks to counter any possible competition.

Thus we read of God in Israel's great declaration of faith: "Listen, O Israel: The LORD is our God, the LORD alone - שְׁמַע יִשְׂרָאֵל יְהוָה

---

[69] I Sa 10:10-11
[70] Exo 29:7
[71] Exo 4:13-16 (NRS)
[72] Gen 2:18 (NRS)

"יְהוָה אֱלֹהֵינוּ יְהוָה אֶחָד:".[73] Later Christian translators rendered the word אֶחָד as the numerical word "one" and attempted to fit this error into the Christian notions of the Trinity – one God and three Gods. This, of course, was never an issue for Jewish translations. Judaism would never have entertained a numerical understanding of the word "one". "Alone" is the only possible meaning of the word, and it has the same effect as the Islamic لا إله إلا الله ("there is no God except Allah").

Only Adam of all the creatures is empowered by God so as to pose as God; and by providing that humankind can only create in pairs God seeks to avert this idolatry, the idolatry of self, which human pride might threaten. The Bible knows that all idols are only projections of prideful humanity. The Bible knows of no God of Evil; the Satan is clearly a creature of God and a servant in the divine court responsible for putting humankind to the test to determine righteousness and humility, a kind of District Attorney.[74] In Scripture, idolatry is a laughable pretension of Adam. God alone is God, for only God is alone.

Assertion 10: That some parts of the Bible will resemble writings from other ages and cultures is not surprising in that human beings often share the same concerns among themselves irrespective of time and culture. This never suggests that the Bible has borrowed from other cultures or copied documents from others.[75] The inevitable difference between biblical documents and those of other cultures lies in the uniqueness of the God of the Bible, which always yields a different interpretation. It is true, however, that the Bible shares a common mind-set or world-view with peoples nearby them. This is, as we shall see further along, the case with the generation of the Wilderness and the people from whom they came – namely Egypt. Israel did not "borrow" or

---

[73] Deu 6:4 (NRS, WTT) This is the real meaning of Israel's profession: "Hear, O Israel: The LORD is our God; the LORD is alone (יְהוָה אֶחָד:).
[74] Just as in the story of Job.
[75] A serious error in post-Wellhausian biblical scholarship which Samuel Sandmel has identified as parallelomania in Samuel Sandmel, "Parallelomania," *Journal of Biblical Literature* 81 (1962): 1-13.

"copy" the ways of Egypt, but the generation of the Wilderness whose forbearers had lived in Egypt for generations would quite naturally view their world, even though now delivered from Egypt, as they had in the land that had been home to them for so long.

Assertion 11: The God we meet in Scripture is completely consistent and reliable, as it says: "The LORD is just in all his ways, and kind in all his doings."[76] Having declared the universe which he created "very good", God does not play games with it. As Einstein once said, "God does not play dice with the universe."[77] The deities of the nations are described as capricious, suspending the natural order to suit their whims, usually by using magic. The God of the Bible is righteous and consistent in his dealings with his creation. He works with and through the "rules" he has put in place. We see this in the wonderful story of Elijah in the cave:

> And He said: 'Go forth, and stand upon the mount before the LORD.' And, behold, the LORD passed by, and a great and strong wind rent the mountains, and broke in pieces the rocks before the LORD; but the LORD was not in the wind; and after the wind an earthquake; but the LORD was not in the earthquake; and after the earthquake a fire; but the LORD was not in the fire; and after the fire a still small voice.[78]

The revelation of the Lord is not through his manipulation of the powers of natural forces, but in near silence and by insinuation. An exception, which proves this rule, concerns one of the battles of Israel in the conquest of the Promised Land:

> Joshua spoke to the LORD; and he (Joshua) said in the sight of Israel, "Sun, stand still at Gibeon, and Moon, in the valley of Aijalon." And the sun stood still, and the moon stopped, until the nation took vengeance on their enemies. Is this not written in the Book of Jashar? The sun stopped in midheaven, and did not hurry to set for about a whole day. There has been no day like it

---

[76] Psa 145:17 (NRS)
[77] Albert Einstein, The Born-Einstein Letters 1916-55.
[78] 1Ki 19:11-12 (JPS)

> before or since, when the LORD heeded a human voice; for the LORD fought for Israel.[79]

That the event is exceptional to the Scriptures is indicated by "there has been no day like it before or since", and that it is from a non-biblical source, the Book of Jashar. It is a one-off and may be an example of the Bible's "obliqueness of style" instances.[80]

In like manner and in accordance with God's great gift of free will to Adam, God does not manipulate people or events to achieve his will. Rather he works through the actions, institutions, decisions, often the foibles, and even the sins of the children of Adam to accomplish his purposes. God is described as patient and longsuffering, allowing humankind to follow its own devices and desires:

> Many years you were patient with them, and warned them by your spirit through your prophets; yet they would not listen. Therefore you handed them over to the peoples of the lands. Nevertheless, in your great mercies you did not make an end of them or forsake them, for you are a gracious and merciful God.[81]

One of the most profound and beautiful statements of this desire by God of working through, often alongside of, normal human life is stated by Joseph when, after the death of his father, his brothers come to him in fear of retribution for their betrayal of him as a young man:

> Realizing that their father was dead, Joseph's brothers said, "What if Joseph still bears a grudge against us and pays us back in full for all the wrong that we did to him?" So they approached Joseph, saying, "Your father gave this instruction before he died, 'Say to Joseph: I beg you, forgive the crime of your brothers and the wrong they did in harming you.' Now therefore please forgive the crime of the servants of the God of your father." Joseph wept when they spoke to him. Then his brothers also wept, fell down before him, and said, "We are here as your

---

[79] Jos 10:12-14 (NRS)
[80] See Herbert C. Brichto, "On Faith and Revelation in the Bible", Hebrew Union College Annual, Vol. XXXIX (1968). Philadelphia: Press of Maurice Jacobs, Inc., pp. 35-53. It may be that Joshua's prayer was to the effect: "Dear Lord, please give us enough day light to finish off this battle completely" – and he did!
[81] Neh 9:30-31 (NRS)

slaves." But Joseph said to them, "Do not be afraid! Am I in the place of God? *Even though you intended to do harm to me, God intended it for good, in order to preserve a numerous people*, as he is doing today.[82]

The point of all this is to say that the God of the Bible does not "fiddle" with his creation or its people; yet he is also involved with that creation and with the children of men. Respectful of the laws governing the universe which he himself created, he does not change them, but uses them to achieve his will. Equally respectful of the freedom he gave to men, he never manipulates humans and their institutions, but accepts to work with and through them. Thus we have the remarkable story of the sin of David with Bath-Sheba, for which David is punished at the time and yet which God uses to bring about the birth of Solomon, King of Israel.[83] God gives us the rope (for he is the source of all things); we choose to make macramé (create good) or a noose for our own hanging. Then God will use both the good and the evil to bring about his own purposes.

We shall see this principle at work below in discussing the Egyptian institutions which the people of Israel brought with them into the wilderness and which God used to create a holy people for himself.

Assertion 12: The Bible's insistence that there is only one God raises the problem of evil and its origins. This is the so-called "theodicy problem"; if God created everything, does this mean that God created evil? If not, and if there is no evil god or devil, how shall we account for it? The Bible makes it clear that evil is a secondary creation. God created everything, but he created man in his own image and likeness, that is, with his own power. Man has the freedom to use this power at his own discretion - humankind can choose the good or evil. Therefore, if evil exists, it is man's abuse of God's power that is its origin.

---

[82] Gen 50:15-20 (NRS)
[83] 2 Samuel 11:1 - 12:24 (NRS)

We humans would like to displace this choice of evil upon some malignant deity to escape our own culpability and have invented many dark lords and kingdoms to escape responsibility; but the Bible is quite clear that "the buck stops with us" and cannot be sidestepped or shifted elsewhere. The devil did not make me do it; it was my choice. This biblical truth is most awkward and difficult.[84]

Assertion 13: The relation of Adam with God in the beginning seems to have been a comfortable conversation between householder and trusted steward: "They heard the sound of the LORD God walking in the garden at the time of the evening breeze, …"[85] if we understand by this that they used to walk together. Such a relationship requires a large measure of humility on the part of the lesser one in the relationship. In fact, humility is a major theme in the Bible, and this virtue characterises those who are closest to God. Frequently, the humble ones (the poor - עָנִי & עָנָו) and the young ones (as with Samuel, David, Gideon, Ruth, Mary and the like), are the ones with whom God speaks more intimately than with others. Of Moses it says: "Now the man Moses was very humble, more so than anyone else on the face of the earth,"[86] and because of this God spoke to Moses not just in dreams and visions of the night, but face to face as one man speaks to his friend.

Likewise, St. Paul says of Jesus:
> Let the same mind be in you that was in Christ Jesus, who, though he was in the form of God, did not regard equality with God as something to be exploited, but emptied himself, taking

---

[84] It is clear that natural disasters are not considered evil by the Bible, for example: "Now there was a great wind, so strong that it was splitting mountains and breaking rocks in pieces before the LORD, but the LORD was not in the wind; and after the wind an earthquake, but the LORD was not in the earthquake; and after the earthquake a fire, but the LORD was not in the fire;" 1Ki 19:11-12 (NRS). See above and Assertion 14 below for further discussion.
[85] Gen 3:8 (NRS)
[86] Num 12:3 (NRS)

the form of a slave, being born in human likeness. And being found in human form, he humbled himself and became obedient to the point of death-- even death on a cross. Therefore God also highly exalted him and gave him the name that is above every name, so that at the name of Jesus every knee should bend, in heaven and on earth and under the earth, and every tongue should confess that Jesus Christ is Lord, to the glory of God the Father.[87]

Moreover, with regard to his people Israel: "He leads the humble in what is right, and teaches the humble his way."[88] The real failure of the Kings of Judah, for example, was with regard to their lack of humility as soon as they achieved power. Arrogance is akin to idolatry in that it exalts the powerful in the face of the majesty of God. The beautiful story of Joseph in Genesis describes a talented but arrogant young man and his becoming humble enough to rise to the position of the saviour of his people. Servanthood and humility are intimately related in Scripture.

Assertion 14: Yet another central and pervasive theme of the Bible is freedom, free will and choice. The Bible relates the work of God and his agents in setting people free and returning them to the freedom and sanity of the choice which they enjoyed in the beginning. The people of Egypt, who have no will save that of Pharaoh, are offered freedom in the great narrative of the Passover. Those who are prisoners of their own passions, of sin, of magic, of the tyrannies and devils of this world or of the idolatrous projections of human egos are, throughout the Bible, the subject of God's intent to release and to free.

Free will and choice are among the gifts of God to humanity in the beginning and are one of the characteristics that separate Adam from all the other animals, themselves only instinctual and incapable of choice. The parable of the two trees[89] in the Garden is the first demonstration of the choice which God makes available to humankind:

---

[87] Phi 2:5-11 (NRS)
[88] Psa 25:9 (NRS)
[89] See my monograph "The Parable of the Two Trees".

> Out of the ground the LORD God made to grow every tree that is pleasant to the sight and good for food, the tree of life also in the midst of the garden, and the tree of the knowledge of good and evil.[90]
>
> And the LORD God commanded the man, "You may freely eat of every tree of the garden; but of the tree of the knowledge of good and evil you shall not eat (לֹא תֹאכַל), for in the day that you eat of it you shall die."[91]
>
> But the serpent said to the woman, "You will not die (if you touch it); for God knows that when you eat of it your eyes will be opened, and you will be like God, knowing good and evil."[92]

The freedom to eat of any tree in the garden is the indication that God gives free will to Adam. The two trees are about human eternal life. Clearly, if you eat from the tree of life, the two of you will live forever. Thus, if you choose to trust in God for the provision of your future life, he gives it to you freely; you need not do anything.

The other tree, the tree of knowledge, gives the knowledge which God did not give to Adam initially, that is, the knowledge of how to make life yourselves. Good and evil are merism, like A to Z or soup to nuts, indicating the whole body of knowledge, and in this case the knowledge of God himself of making life, the holiest of God's powers. However, God knows that if Adam were to create life, Adam could not create worlds for that life to inhabit if Adam's offspring were to eat of the tree of life as well and live forever. Overpopulation could not be sustained and chaos would follow. Thus God's warning to Adam, "The downside of eating from this tree is mortality; you must die in your generation to make room for what you create. You must be satisfied with a future life through your children and their children, each generation dying to make room for the next."

The word "die" is first used in the Bible with regard to this alert from God: "but of the tree of the knowledge of good and evil you

---

[90] Gen 2:9 (NRS)
[91] Gen 2:16-17(NRS)
[92] Gen 3:4-5 (NRS)

shall not eat, for in the day that you eat of it you shall die.'"[93] This use of "surely die" (מוֹת תָּמוּת:) should in no way be construed as God's creation or devising of death. This would be contrary to the principle of life built into the creation itself. Rather, "to die" here and often elsewhere has the sense of "become mortal", that is, to become subject to the principle of mortality in which individuals are only a part of a particular generation which will pass and give way to another cohort of the living. We note that even mortality is a choice of humanity and never a divine imposition.

It is important that we understand that God did not forbid eating from this tree; he simply charged them, "Don't eat from it, because it has the side effect of mortality." To have forbidden it we would have a God creating at least the temptation to sin and the proposal of a false choice. Such an interpretation would suggest that God likes to trick his children. Nothing could be further from the truth. The prior question to the parable of the trees is, "Why do people die?" The simple answer is, "To prevent overpopulation". The gift of sex is God's sharing his most profound and holy power with Adam and the choice to use this power is Adam's. Death is not a punishment for anything but a normal part of human life which is engaged in procreation. We, the offspring of Adam, must be grateful that the couple chose the gift of procreation, else we would not be here at all. If there is a "fall" here – and there is certainly not – it is truly "felix culpa", a fortunate fall indeed for those beyond the first two in the garden.

Because this story is a parable of "everyman", we can detect in it the great humour of the Bible here which is often missed by those whose ponderous theological concerns stifle the lightheartedness of the Biblical narrative.

The misinterpretation of this parable of the two trees can lead to some dire consequences for biblical interpretation, since much of the Bible has to do with life and the unqualified goodness of God's gifts in creation. It has been customary in some circles to interpret

---

[93] Gen 2:17 (NRS)

God's warning about the tree of knowledge as a commandment of the order of the commandments from Sinai, i.e. Thou shalt not...! Thus, the eating from the tree is a sin and thus sex is a sin, historically the original sin. This is misguided indeed, for it makes God responsible for setting Adam up to sin; and it suggests that God's holy gift of giving life is associated with sin and death, rather than joy and life. It is no wonder that sex and sin go together in these circles, and that God is separated from his holy gift of creating life!

Furthermore, such an interpretation invites the appearance of an evil God (usually identified with the snake in the tree) so that we end up with a dualism of gods, one of which, the evil god, is attached to the physical and sexual world; the other, the good god, becomes associated with the "spiritual", non-physical world. This ancient heresy of Manichaeism continues in popular belief to the present time (as suggested in Assertion 9, above).[94]

The truth is that the so-called "curses" attached to the eating from the tree of knowledge are only restrictive consequences of mortality and not punishments for sin. They are simply the limitations upon human procreation. In short, humans are indeed like God in being able to create life, but there are differences between human procreation and God's creation of life. God does it effortlessly and without pain; humans endure pain in the whole enterprise ("with labour you will do your procreating"). In short, you will be like God, but you will not be God! The same is true with the life created. The life God creates endures forever; the life Adam makes has a limit and an end. Furthermore, the restrictions on human procreation are clearly evident and a part of normal human experience.

There is a restatement of God's limit upon humankind in terms of human mortality in a statement after the flood: Then the LORD

---

[94] This misunderstanding of the eating from the tree of knowledge has probably gone further than most in bringing the biblical message into disrepute and making it laughable.

said, "My spirit shall not abide in man for ever, for he is flesh, but his days shall be a hundred and twenty years."[95] This is not seen as a punishment or in any way vindictive on God's part; simply a restatement of the fact of a significant difference between God and humankind in terms of power and ability. While God shares his power of creating life, only God can create worlds for that life to inhabit. Adam is created in the image and likeness of God, but not entirely. God's creation is unlimited; the doings of humans have limitations of time and space.

We are told of this limitation on human creation in Genesis, where we read: "Then the LORD God said, "It is not good that the man should be alone; I will make him a helper fit for him."[96] The "fit helper" for Adam means a fit partner for procreation. And since we have suggested that the "good" of creation is good for God, "not good" is also not good for God. It is not good for God in that if Adam is created in the very image and likeness of God in power and authority and Adam is alone as God is alone, Adam will soon begin to think of himself as God (the fundamental sin of man). Adam is always plural and societal.

The idea of individual life after death is quite foreign to the Old Testament. While the ancient Egyptians did have some ideas of an of individual's life going on after the death of the body, this had very much to do with the manipulation of powers by magic, and human magic at that. The Book of the Dead, the embalming of dead bodies and the manipulation of powers to escape the dangers facing the dead had nothing to do with a God who creates and favours life. This "afterlife" was dependent upon the keeping and ministrations by the living of "houses of the dead". It seems to have been pretty much restricted in its promise to the upper classes and the rich. It is at best a shadowy life and very much dependent on the ministrations of the living. Grave robbers and those who erased the name of the dead were able to abort this immortality at will. Immortality in Egypt seems to have been a rather florid

---
[95] Gen 6:3 (RSV)
[96] Gen 2:18(RSV)

poetic concept than a reality. While gods were featured in the drama, no god gave or maintained life. There is some evidence that even the Egyptians shared the Middle Eastern idea of life continuing through the generations.

The Bible does not speculate on the so-called "afterlife". There are a few accounts in both Old and New Testaments about the raising of the dead to life, but they are in every case a restoration of the dead to a continuation of their previous lives in this world. Nowhere is there a speculation concerning their situation between the time of "dying" and their being revived. Presumably, too, all of them (including Lazarus) died again.[97] Only one story in the Old Testament even hints at the situation of the dead, and that is the story of the raising of the dead Samuel by the witch of Endor on behalf of the terrified (and depressed) King Saul.

> The king said to her, "Have no fear; what do you see?" The woman said to Saul, "I see a divine being (אֱלֹהִים) coming up out of the ground." He said to her, "What is his appearance?" She said, "An old man is coming up; he is wrapped in a robe." So Saul knew that it was Samuel, and he bowed with his face to the ground, and did obeisance. Then Samuel said to Saul, "Why have you disturbed me by bringing me up?" Saul answered, "I am in great distress, for the Philistines are warring against me, and God has turned away from me and answers me no more, either by prophets or by dreams; so I have summoned you to tell me what I should do."[98]

The spectre of Samuel is that of the old man as he was when he died – there is no change. Samuel speaks of being disturbed or agitated, but there is nothing in this to suggest anything about his dead state other than he might be at rest, a rest which the magic of the witch has agitated. Samuel is recognisable to Saul and addressed Saul's problem, suggesting no loss of identity of the dead, and his irascibility seems to be consistent with the personality of the prophet before he died. There also seems to be some presumption that the dead Samuel can look into the future

---

[97] Joh 12:10
[98] 1Sa 28:13-15 (NRS)

(though this may also attend on his having been a prophet). But this is all the speculation of an afterlife in the Bible.

From the time of the patriarchs, the usual description of death is "being gathered to one's fathers": "Abraham breathed his last and died in a good old age, an old man and full of years, and was gathered to his people."[99]   The exceptions are Jacob and Joseph who died without access to a family burying place and who are mummified in the Egyptian fashion and carried back to Canaan with the Exodus:

> "When Jacob ended his charge to his sons, he drew up his feet into the bed, breathed his last, and was gathered to his people."[100]
> "My father made me swear an oath; he said, 'I am about to die. In the tomb that I hewed out for myself in the land of Canaan, there you shall bury me.' Now therefore let me go up, so that I may bury my father; then I will return."[101]
> "And Joseph died, being one hundred ten years old; he was embalmed and placed in a coffin in Egypt."[102]

Thus we learn that "being gathered to the fathers" amounts to being placed in the family tomb. Nothing is said or even hinted about an afterlife.

Moses himself, the greatest prophet of Israel, died unobserved by anyone, and is presumed to have been tended at his end only by God himself. It is recorded that he died and was buried in an unmarked grave:

> Then Moses, the servant of the LORD, died there in the land of Moab, at the LORD's command. He was buried in a valley in the land of Moab, opposite Beth-peor, but no one knows his burial place to this day.[103]

He does not even merit the dramatic translation to heaven as was enjoyed by the prophet Elijah in the fiery chariot.

---

[99] Gen. 25:8 (NRS). See also Gen. 35:29; Gen. 49:33
[100] Gen 49:33 (NRS)
[101] Gen 50:5 (NRS)
[102] Gen. 50:26 (NRS)
[103] Deu 34:5-6 (NRS)

Clearly, the Old Testament views death as "going to sleep" – and that is all. All that remains of the individual is that which is remembered by others who are still alive, most particularly the family of the deceased, or, as with the Kings of Judah and Israel, that which is written in official archives about them:

> "Then David slept with his ancestors, and was buried in the city of David."[104]
>
> "Menahem slept with his ancestors, and his son Pekahiah succeeded him."[105]
>
> "For David, after he had served his own generation by the will of God, fell asleep, was buried with his fathers, and saw corruption;"[106]
>
> "Now the rest of the acts of Josiah, and all that he did, are they not written in the Book of the Annals of the Kings of Judah?"[107]
>
> "Now Absalom in his lifetime had taken and set up for himself a pillar that is in the King's Valley, for he said, 'I have no son to keep my name in remembrance'; he called the pillar by his own name. It is called Absalom's Monument to this day."[108]

The last verse about Absalom gives us real insight into the Bible's understanding of immortality achieved through the male child of an in Israelite man. Absalom has no son so that he must set up a stone in this world with his name so that he might remain "alive" in the world of the living through the remembrance of his name (אֵין־לִי בֵן בַּעֲבוּר הַזְכִּיר שְׁמִי).[109]

More important than the body, which goes to sleep and becomes corrupted, is the person's name (שֵׁם), which is the person's reality, identity and life. The "name" corresponds roughly to our own word "soul". That reality which remains in the world after a person's death is most usually the son of the deceased, who is called the זִכָּרוֹן or the (living) memory or memorial of the deceased and who, by keeping the deceased's name alive, in fact keeps the dead alive in this world. To "honour father and mother" is to keep

---

[104] 1Ki 2:10 (NRS)
[105] 2Ki 15:22 (NRS)
[106] Act 13;36 (NKJ)
[107] 2Ki 23:28 (NRS)
[108] 2Sa 18:18 (NRS)
[109] 2Sa 18:18 (WTT)

their names alive in remembrance, from generation to generation. Poor Absalom has no son and must be satisfied with a stone with his name carved on it.

We can say, then, that while the body sleeps in the corruption of death, the deceased's life continues in the living and life-giving memorial of the son, grandson, great-grandson and so on. To fail to have a son, then, is to have one's name obliterated from this world. The great pains to which biblical folks go to have a son at any cost (even incest[110] and prostitution[111]) is therefore understandable[112]. The more sons, the greater the guarantee of immortality.

All of the above is given to show that the God of the Bible deals with the present world rather than some hazy and dark speculation about another world where the dead live or subsist onwards. And this is precisely due to the fact that the Bible is about God and not about humanity or any individual human.

Even the rise of the doctrine of resurrection entails no description of the condition of the dead before they are raised. The death of Stephen the protomartyr, even as he is attesting to the resurrection of Jesus is described: "Then he knelt down and cried out with a loud voice, 'Lord, do not charge them with this sin.' And when he had said this, he fell asleep."[113]

Human immortality[114] will be defined through the family – each generation will be the living end of all the generations of the

---

[110] Gen 19:32-36
[111] Gen 38:14ff
[112] This is also the underlying reason for the command: "You shall not lie with a male as with a woman; it is an abomination." Lev 18:22 (NRS)
[113] Act 7:60 (NKJ)
[114] The word "immortality" here and elsewhere in this work is never used in the philosophical or spiritual sense of the Greeks, but has a rather more vague sense of eternality in keeping with the Hebrew's rather poor concept of specific times and verb tenses. The Hebrew word is לְעֹלָם and suggests "on into this age". The plural, "ages" is used of God's eternality and suggests on into "ages of ages", (עוֹלָמִים). Perhaps we

family who have gone before, and by remembering those generations in the present will keep them alive in the present. Each generation is the "living quick" of the generations before it. This is the meaning of Boaz's actions in the Book of Ruth:

> Then Boaz said, "The day you acquire the field from the hand of Naomi, you are also acquiring Ruth the Moabite, the widow of the dead man, to maintain the dead man's name on his inheritance."[115], and
> I have also acquired Ruth the Moabite, the wife of Mahlon, to be my wife, to maintain the dead man's name on his inheritance, in order that the name of the dead may not be cut off from his kindred and from the gate of his native place; today you are witnesses.[116]

This honouring of the generations is probably behind David's visit to Bethlehem:

> Jonathan answered Saul, "David earnestly asked leave of me to go to Bethlehem; he said, 'Let me go; for our family is holding a sacrifice in the city, and my brother has commanded me to be there. So now, if I have found favor in your sight, let me get away, and see my brothers.' For this reason he has not come to the king's table."[117]

It is clearly the intent behind the commandment: "Honour thy father and thy mother" – that is, after they have died.

Assertion 15: Yet another consequence of God's gifts to Adam of free will is the origin of sin in the Bible. As has been noted above in Assertion 10, the Bible never connects God with evil, its creation or its doing. This includes the origins of sin. While some commentators seek to show that sin in the Bible is connected with God's providing temptations to sin by the malignancy of his

---

would be better served by the word "on-going". The Old Testament prejudice against Egypt and its religion of the "good life" in this world and its belief that by magic it can also assure that same "good life" into immortality and after the grave are always rejected, and particularly because of the magic involved. The Bible frequently mocks the arrogances of Egypt. One does not need to look far to see those same arrogances in today's world.

[115] Rut 4:5 (NRS)
[116] Rut 4:10 (NRS)
[117] 1Sa 20:28-29 (NRS)

creatures, for example the serpent in the Tree of Knowledge from Good to Evil or some rather convoluted descriptions of fallen angels and other celestial creatures, the Bible will not ever entertain any god-like creature with the power to compete with himself and his divinity by introducing anything into his creation having to do with the "not-Good" or any kind of evil.

While a Devil or Satan remains the fantasy of medieval superstitions as well as more modern fundamentalist religious imaginations, they in no way belong to the Bible.[118] From time to time in Israel's religious practise, there was also a more florid development of folk- angelology, based usually upon Jacob's wrestling with the angel in Genesis.[119] Such a flirtation with angels, however, never had the intent of setting up an alternative power to God's own, either for good or evil.

The only creature to have the ability for running contrary to the Good established by God in the creation is Adam. We are told that only Adam is created in the image and likeness of God, implying God-like powers and abilities. God created Adam with these powers in order that Adam might carry out the task assigned to him in the beginning, namely that care of God's creation and the task of keeping it in the order which God calls "the Good". Yet for Adam to have unfettered control of his appropriate sphere of activity as caretaker of the Garden which is creation and the life in it, Adam must have the freedom to choose, implied by the intent of God in Genesis 1:28 that Adam have "dominion".

---

[118] When the Bible does mention the "Satan, in the Book of Job, and in the Temptation of Jesus in the wilderness", it (he) s only as a functionary of God's own Court where the Satan is the official who, in the United States judicial system, would be called the Attorney General and whose function is to present cases for potential trial. There is nothing evil about him. The temptations of this official are more properly judicial tests and never temptations to sin. In the case of Jesus, the Tester is a part of himself, proposing two choices, both of which are possible. In modern parlance we would speak of a "good" conscience or a "bad" conscience.
[119] Gen 32:24ff.

The ability of Adam to depart from the agenda of "the Good" arises from the freedom to choose derived from the power of "dominion". Since the Bible is not historical, sin (doing the "not Good") is never seen as original in an historic sense, as originating with some Ur-Adam. Rather, it is more appropriate to speak of the inclination to sin as "fundamental" to humankind generally, now and in the past.

Further, since the Old Testament does cannot speak of ontologies and the "nature" of things (having no present tense of the verb "to be"), sin is a chosen behaviour of humankind and never something "essential" or indelible to human "nature". The parable that describes the actual choice of humankind to go contrary to the Good and engage in sinning is the Parable of the Twins.

As with most of the Bible's parable-narrative, the names of the characters have great significance for the narrative itself. Cain's name means "jealousy, anger and a rod for beating".[120] Abel's name means "a puff of wind" or "pride", indicating his passing role as the prideful antagonist to his brother. The boys are twins (one conception, two births[121]), suggesting that jealousy and pride are but two sides of the single human coin. They enter into a sacrificing contest with each other to determine which one of them God loves the most, a pointless exercise in which God has no part at all. As with most human adversarial contests to determine a "winner" and the one who is "the best", they make the rules and they decide the winner and the loser. Abel here is the proud winner and Cain the jealous and very angry loser.[122]

Cain sinks into a blue funk over his brother's "triumph" and he is confronted by God – who is quite neutral in all this – with the question: "Why are you so down-in-the-mouth and angry, Cain?"

---

[120] "So after they had gathered, Pilate said to them, "Whom do you want me to release for you, Jesus Barabbas or Jesus who is called the Messiah? For he realized that it was out of *jealousy* that they had handed him over." (Mat 27:17-18 NRS).
[121] Gen.4;1-2
[122] We have only to look at wars and football matches today to know the truth of this sibling struggle!

Cain's charge against God, "You love him more than you love me" is Cain's childish and outrageous reply. God's response to Cain and to each of us presents us with a significant choice for every human:

> If you do well (אִם־תֵּיטִיב), will you not be accepted? And if you do not do well (וְאִם לֹא תֵיטִיב) sin (חַטָּאת) is lurking at the door; its desire is for you, but you must master it (תִּמְשָׁל־בּוֹ)."[123]

The choice is, as usual, given by two "ifs". "Do well" is to be understood as "do the Good". The choice to Cain is clear and unmistakable. "If in this situation with your brother you do the Good, Cain, you are always acceptable to me and all will be well. But if you do not do the Good, sin will be the result and it will overwhelm you. Most important, you must gain mastery over sin."

This is the first actual reference to sin in the Bible. Clearly, sin is presented as a choice of response to a situation. Sin is not a thing, nor is it inevitable. This is the true "original sin" or, as it might be better termed, the "fundamental sin" for all humankind. It is defined as a failure to do "the Good". And what is "the Good"? While we will not have a statement of the Law for many generations, it would appear that God's assumption is that the sons of men will know the Good without its being spelled out or codified. Since God has declared about his creation from the very outset that it is "Good", we must, as Cain was urged to do, search the creation of its meaning.

We have already shown the four principles governing the creation and its workings according to God's "Good": 1) maintaining the boundaries; 2) affirming the value of each of the parts; 3) keeping the balance between the parts; and 4) affirming life as the prime directive of the universe. Thus, Cain is given a choice of keeping the boundaries between himself and Abel - or not. He is able, if he will but look, to see the God-createdness of Abel just as his own (they are, after all, twins) - or not. He is invited to choose his brother as himself and maintain the balance between the two of

---

[123] Gen 4:7 (NRS)

them (the true meaning of human love) - or not. Moreover, he can hold as precious as his own the life of his brother - or not. He can choose to do the "Good" with his brother – or not.

The parable continues: "Cain said to his brother Abel, 'Let us go out to the field.' And when they were in the field, Cain rose up against his brother Abel, and killed (read, "murdered") him."[124] Having perceived his brother as a rival rather than a brother, Cain chooses to remove his brother from the equation on the grounds that he has no responsibility for his brother. "Am I my brother's keeper?" he demands. He chooses to sin and God asks him: "Do you know what you have done"? Thus God's question is not to explore the action of Cain so much as to raise the issue of the consequences to the creation itself of the introduction of sin into the world. God's outrage is clear: "I have heard your brother's blood (life) screaming 'Bloody murder' from the very ground!" All creation is offended and repulsed by this action and Cain's choice for murder.[125]

Cain's offence against God's righteousness and the very fabric of the "Good" with which God created the universe is unspeakable. Like a stone thrown into a lake, the rings continue to move outward to the very limits. Nor can Cain go back and undo what he has perpetrated or remedy it in any way. The gardener has set in motion the destruction of the garden entrusted to his care. All hell has broken loose. The exercise of the free will entrusted to Adam has made available a choice of sin. God gave Cain, as he does us, all the rope we require; but Cain chose to make a noose for his own hanging rather than macramé.[126] God gives only the

---

[124] Gen 4:8 (NRS)
[125] Here we learn that the real and profound original sin is murder and all its consequences rather than some sexual offence.
[126] It is a given in biblical religion that God creates and is in control of everything. Yet equally fundamental to the Bible is that sin exists and God did not create it. This paradox is a radical result of the Bible's absolute monotheism; but it begs the question of the origin of sin. The story of the struggle between God and Pharaoh over the people of Israel includes the disturbing statement: "But the LORD hardened the heart of Pharaoh, and he would not listen to them, just as the LORD had spoken to Moses." (Exo

gifts; humankind chooses to use them for the Good of creation or for sin. Humankind, and no one else, is the author of sin; and sadly, I am Cain.

Without question, Cain has committed a capital offence and simple justice requires a capital punishment – Cain's life for Abel's. This would be a righteous sentence and in no sense would it be a matter of vengeance. God should terminate Cain's life and put an end to the human experiment. It is only fair! Imagine our surprise when we hear the sentence of the divine Judge:
> And now you are cursed from the ground, which has opened its mouth to receive your brother's blood from your hand. When you till the ground, it will no longer yield to you its strength; you will be a fugitive and a wanderer on the earth."[127]

We are astonished at the sentence – banishment rather than death. Can the Creator of heaven and earth, the righteous judge, be so unfair as to spare Cain's life? He deserves death. A clue to understanding what seems to be an outrage on God's part is for us to recall that death is never a part of God's creation or of God's plan for his creation. Death is really only mortality and not a punishment for anything. God does not do death any more than he does sin. In fact, God does not punish – he simply allows the punishment which is implicit in the sin to take effect. This, once again, is the Bible's oblique style which permits God to be in charge without having to do anything negative. In short, sin entails its own punishment, and since man is the sinner, so man brings the punishment on himself. It is never God's doing. "We might be

---

9:12 NRS). Does Scripture really mean that God forced Pharaoh to sin? The answer is, of course, not at all. This is the Bible's oblique way of stating the paradox: God is the source of Pharaoh's power but the sinful choice of using that power for evil and to oppose God himself lies in the hands of Pharaoh. Thus, free will is guaranteed to Pharaoh the man while absolute power is reserved to God. Paradox is an untidy and very hard concept for our modern, scientific minds. The Bible manages it quite well due to the nature of the Hebrew language.
This most important and equally difficult problem of biblical interpretation is brilliantly addressed in a little-known but most significant article by my teacher, Rabbi Dr. Herbert C. Brichto (a"h), "On Faith and Revelation in the Bible", op. cit.
[127] Gen 4:11-12 (NRS)

tempted to say, "What goes around comes around." If you are dumb enough to play on the roof and fall off, it is not God's (or even gravity's) fault.

To understand how this works in the parable of Cain, we must understand something about ancient life that is different from our own (though even some cultures of modern times still retain some elements of it). It is particularly important in nomadic cultures. In nomadic cultures, one lives in safety in the bosom of one's family encampment, protected by the family or extended family (sometimes the tribe). Every family has a mark or badge or sign which identifies every member of the family/tribe as one who belongs to the family and enjoys its protection. This could be a ring, a badge, a special headdress or part of a headdress – much as a soldier today wears a uniform or badge on the uniform that identifies the unit to which the soldier belongs and where the soldier is "at home".

This mark becomes critical when any individual leaves the safety of home for a journey on the open road where that individual is particularly at risk of robbers and those who would murder for gain. The mark tells anyone who meets the traveler that that person belongs to a family. More specifically, the mark says of the wandering individual that at home he has someone called his "redeemer of blood"[128] (גֹּאֵל(וֹ) הַדָּם), referred to as his "brother" (אָח). If the travelling family member is murdered on the road, it is the duty of the "brother" to apprehend the murderer and to kill him. The purpose of this is to prevent a blood-feud. When the brother kills the murderer, the price is paid for the life of the dead traveller. What is even more important is that the would-be murderer, seeing the mark on the traveller, knows that he has a blood-redeemer brother who will surely pursue him to the death, and he will leave the traveller alone. This, in fact, prevents murder in the first place.

---

[128] גֹּאֵל(וֹ) הַדָּם, avenger of bloodshed (who, by killing the murderer of one's relative, clears away the crime) 1K 16$_{11}$.

Now we return to the punishment of Cain. God condemns him to become a wandering sojourner outside the bosom of the family:

> When you till the ground, it will no longer yield to you its strength; you will be a fugitive and a wanderer on the earth." Cain said to the LORD, "My punishment is greater than I can bear! Today you have driven me away from the soil, and I shall be hidden from your face; I shall be a fugitive and a wanderer on the earth, and anyone who meets me may kill me."[129]

We wonder at first at Cain's ingratitude, "My punishment is greater than I can bear!" Apparently, he has, gotten away with murder and has suffered only banishment. Then we read further, "and anyone who meets me may kill me (with impunity)". We reply, "But you have a brother, an avenger or redeemer back at home who will be your keeper. Where is he?" And Cain must reply, "I murdered him." "Are you your brother's keeper, Cain?" Yes, just as he was my keeper before I took away his life." "What is the solution to your problem, Cain?" "There isn't one. I have brought about my own punishment and death." "Is God punishing you, Cain?" "No, I have brought the punishment upon myself. I have murdered my twin brother and so murdered myself and all humanity."

The seeds of punishment are embedded in the sin itself, and sin is the choice of Cain, the son of Adam (or the son of Man).

We must now deal with the tag at the end of God's warning to Cain at the beginning of the incident with his brother: "sin is lurking at the door; its desire is for you, *but you must master it* (תִּמְשָׁל־בּוֹ)."[130] The force of God's statement to Cain is at least a strong imperative, though, like the warning concerning the Tree of Knowledge, it is not a commandment. It has the force of "the choice is completely yours" or "over to you, Cain". It would be very hard to make a case that Cain cannot "master it" or that there could be any impediment attached to Cain's "nature" that would

---

[129] Gen 4:12-14 (NRS)
[130] Gen 4:7 (NRS)

prevent his being able to master sin. The text of Scripture is very clear. "Cain, you have a choice and you really should choose against sin and to do 'the Good'."

This little phrase raises the whole spectre of the controversy between Pelagius and Augustine and his often-Predestinarian colleagues and followers (c. 400-529 AD). The problem here is that both Pelagius and Augustine identify original sin with the eating of the Tree of Knowledge, they both understand man to have a "nature", and they both use their political influence to have the other declared "heretic".

They are both very much like Cain and Abel in the biblical parable – Augustine "wins" and Pelagius "loses". While orthodoxy follows Augustine, one wonders seriously if the Church is any wiser in dealing with the reality of sin by following him or his disciples.[131] It is clear that Pelagius nearly "won" in the East and in Ireland. If only we can peek over their controversy and ask again, "What is God's revelation in this phrase, 'You must master sin'?" Perhaps he means just what he says, "You can and you should choose to do 'the Good' which I have laid out for you in my Word.

Assertion 16: God has alerted Cain of the consequences of his choice not "to do the Good". Sin is the consequence and inherent in the sin is its punishment, namely death. We have noted that death is not God's doing or his punishment; it follows on from the choice. And because the sin is murder, the compensatory punishment must be Cain's life for his brother's. Just as Abel would have been Cain's redeemer, his "redeemer in blood", his הַדָּם גֹּא(וֹ)ל, so having murdered his redeemer Cain is now beyond redemption.

And as Cain says, "The punishment is greater than I can bear" – in

---

[131] One does wonder sometimes if Augustine's enthusiasm is the work of the Holy Spirit or of St. Monica, his mother.

short, I cannot pay and still live myself. The price is more than I have! As St. Paul tersely states it: "For the wages of sin is death."[132] If there is to be any solution to Cain's problem, it must be provided by someone other than himself and another who can give life to replace the one Cain cannot provide, for Cain has committed the capital crime *par excellence.*

Clearly, it is only God who can create life and who could provide the price of Cain's redemption. The problem with this solution is that it is God who is ultimately offended by the destruction of life, for the murder of Abel runs counter to God's love of and commitment to righteousness and justice.

God is presented foremost in Scripture as a just God: "The Rock, his work is perfect, and all his ways are just. A faithful God, without deceit, just and upright is he."[133] "Righteousness and justice are the foundation of your throne; steadfast love and faithfulness go before you."[134] "I put on righteousness, and it clothed me; my justice was like a robe and a turban."[135] God created the heavens and the earth according to his righteousness and he continues to hold them up with justice and equity. For God to supply a remedy for Cain, he must be willing to forego his love of and commitment to justice and righteousness.

We have posited that Adam has free will as a gift from God. If we presume that God shares with Adam that which is his own, we must also presume the free will of God and that he too makes choices freely. Yet how can we say that God chooses and yet he is always consistent, unchanging and ever constant, unlike the gods of the nations who are capricious and act according to their whims? The answer lies in his name:

---

[132] Rom 6:23 (NRS)
[133] Deu 32:4 (NRS)
[134] Psa 89:14 (NRS)
[135] Job 29:14 (NRS)

> The LORD passed before him, and proclaimed, "The LORD, the LORD, a God merciful and gracious, slow to anger, and abounding in steadfast love and faithfulness,
> keeping steadfast love for the thousandth generation, forgiving iniquity and transgression and sin, yet by no means clearing the guilty, but visiting the iniquity of the parents upon the children and the children's children, to the third and the fourth generation."[136]

God is both righteous and just ("yet by no means clearing the guilty") *and* he is merciful ("a God merciful and gracious"). However, justice and mercy are antithetical to each other and mutually exclusive.

Repeatedly, the God of the Bible turns from the way of justice and righteousness to show mercy:

> No one who conceals transgressions will prosper, but one who confesses and forsakes them will obtain mercy.[137]
> Let the wicked forsake their way, and the unrighteous their thoughts; let them return to the LORD, that he may have mercy on them, and to our God, for he will abundantly pardon.[138]
> <To the leader. A Psalm of David, when the prophet Nathan came to him, after he had gone in to Bathsheba.> Have mercy on me, O God, according to your steadfast love; according to your abundant mercy blot out my transgressions.[139]
> Have mercy upon us, O LORD, have mercy upon us, for we have had more than enough of contempt.[140]

It is as though God, if he is to persist in the human experiment, must make the concession to depart from his great love of justice and righteousness and exercise mercy so that Adam might be able to endure.

Every choice between two ways involves some pain and sacrifice. Choosing one way means that I give up the other; I cannot have my cake and eat it too. This is true for God as well. By choosing

---

[136] Exo 34:6-7 (NRS)
[137] Pro 28:13 (NRS)
[138] Isa 55:7 (NRS)
[139] Psa 51:1 (NRS)
[140] Psa 123:3 (NRS)

mercy, he gives up the justice that he loves. The God of the Bible is extraordinary and unique in his willingness to sacrifice what is precious to himself for the sake of a humankind that chooses to turn against him.

The normal course of justice runs thus: If someone transgresses the right order of things and is caught in the offence, he is taken before the judge; the judge determines innocence or guilt; if guilty, the person is given a punishment by which the righteous order is restored; the end and fulfilment of justice is the carrying out of the punishment.

Yet if the guilty party, having been sentenced, throws himself on the mercy of the court *with sorrow for the transgression*, the judge may, at his own discretion and for no reason other than the sorrow of the offender, interpose mercy between the declaration of the just punishment and the actual carrying out of the punishment. Thus, mercy is an intrusion into the normal course of justice and in fact actually undoes justice. Mercy can never be demanded, only pleaded for. Moreover, mercy is offensive to justice in that it circumvents it and its normal course.

What seems to move God to change his mind and exercise mercy is very evidently the repentance of his people: "If we confess our sins, he who is faithful and just will forgive us our sins and cleanse us from all unrighteousness."[141] Moses' intercession to spare the people after the sin of the golden calf is instructive:
> The LORD said to Moses, "I have seen this people, how stiff-necked they are. Now let me alone, so that my wrath may burn hot against them and I may consume them; and of you I will make a great nation."[142]
> So Moses returned to the LORD and said, "Alas, this people has sinned a great sin; they have made for themselves gods of gold.
> On the next day Moses said to the people, "You have sinned a great sin. But now I will go up to the LORD; perhaps I can make atonement for your sin." So Moses returned to the LORD and

---
[141] 1Jo 1:9 (NRS)
[142] Exo 32:9-10 (NRS)

> said, "Alas, this people has sinned a great sin; they have made for themselves gods of gold (the confession). But now, if you will only forgive their sin (the plea for mercy) -- but if not, blot me out of the book that you have written."[143]

Because sin is a choice ("*if* you do not do the good"), choosing differently with sorrow invites God to choose mercy rather than the just punishment of the sin. Such a change of mind on God's part is even called God's "repentance":

> Why should the Egyptians say, 'It was with evil intent that he brought them out to kill them in the mountains, and to consume them from the face of the earth'? Turn from your fierce wrath; change your mind (repent) and do not bring disaster on your people. And the LORD changed his mind (repented) about the disaster that he planned to bring on his people.[144]

In the case of Cain God chooses to act with mercy and not carrying out the just sentence of capital punishment. Clearly, God chooses mercy over his beloved justice, even in the face of the gravest sin of murder. This choice of God to override justice in favour of mercy seems to be occasioned by a turning or repentance of Cain from his sin with sorrow and awareness of the sin. With Cain the confession and repentance seem to be his sudden awareness of what he has done to himself by murdering his brother and then the horror expressed by "anyone who finds me will kill me." Our compassion for Cain needs to be our own relief that God does act with mercy towards Cain, for we are, each of us, Cain himself. "All have sinned and fall short of the glory of God;"[145]

The parable of Cain and Abel continues after Cain expresses his despair over his situation. "Anyone who comes upon me (in the open country and without a sign of belonging) will murder me." "I am a dead man for certain." The most remarkable thing about this story of the beginning of original sin is that it does not end with the punishment that is Cain's due for murder. There is no capital

---

[143] Exo 32:30-32 (NRS)
[144] Exo 32:12, 14 (NRS)
[145] Rom 3:23 (NRS)

punishment given for this committing of sin. Somewhere in Cain's response, God discerns repentance and so changes his mind about Cain:

> Then the LORD said to him, "Not so! Whoever kills Cain will suffer a sevenfold vengeance." And the LORD put a mark[146] on Cain, so that no one who came upon him would kill him.[147]

In fact, the Lord has given Cain God's own "family mark" and taken the place of Abel as Cain's redeemer. This mark or sign of belonging to God's own "family", probably a cross as the last letter of the Hebrew alphabet, seems to have played a part in identifying God's particular agents.

The family mark of the people of Israel, beginning with Abraham, is the mark of circumcision:

> You shall circumcise the flesh of your foreskins, and it shall be a sign of the covenant between me and you. Throughout your generations every male among you shall be circumcised when he is eight days old, including the slave born in your house and the one bought with your money from any foreigner who is not of your offspring. Both the slave born in your house and the one bought with your money must be circumcised. So shall my covenant be in your flesh an everlasting covenant. Any uncircumcised male who is not circumcised in the flesh of his foreskin shall be cut off from his people; he has broken my covenant."[148]

And again, for the people who had come through the wilderness and were about to enter the Promised Land, God's family place:

> So it was their children, whom he raised up in their place, that Joshua circumcised; for they were uncircumcised, because they had not been circumcised on the way.[149]

The matter of the mark of redemption or protection probably lies behind the story of Elisha and the bears:

---

[146] תָּו: sf. תָּוִי: name of last letter of Heb. alphabet, orig. in shape of X or +: **mark** Ez 9$_{4•6}$, (one's own) **mark** or **signature** (confirming a document)
[147] Gen 4:15 (NRS)
[148] Gen 17:11-14 (NRS)
[149] Jos 5:7 (NRS)

> He went up from there to Bethel; and while he was going up on the way, some small boys came out of the city and jeered at him, saying, "Go away, baldhead! Go away, baldhead!" When he turned around and saw them, he cursed them in the name of the LORD. Then two she-bears came out of the woods and mauled forty-two of the boys.[150]

The prophets seemed to have had a tonsure from forehead to mid-crown (the taunt of the children about being a "baldy") and it is possible, since they lived alone or in prophetic schools and had no families, that they bore God's sign on their tonsured area, marking them as God's special servants and under his special protection.

The special mark of the faithful in Ezekiel 9 is also a sign of a special membership in the family of God that has an apotropaic function for those bearing it. It seems most likely that this same mark was meant by Jesus when he declares: "He called the crowd with his disciples, and said to them, 'If any want to become my followers, let them deny themselves and take up their cross and follow me.'"[151]

Adam's (humankind's) sin in Scripture is irremediable by Adam himself. Only God provides the remedy out of his willingness to show mercy. A penitential plea for mercy is in fact a cry of humility; and God loves humility.

> All these things my hand has made, and so all these things are mine, says the LORD. But this is the one to whom I will look, to the humble and contrite in spirit, who trembles at my word.[152]

Assertion 17: The major concern of the biblical narrative is the alienation of humankind from God who created it and from each other, an alienation which begins with Cain's choice to ignore the "Good". While the story of Cain ends with Cain's forgiveness by God and a healing of the breach, the subsequent parables reveal what becomes the habitual inclination (יֵצֶר) of humankind to turn away from God and against each other. We must note that this

---

[150] 2Ki 2:23-24 (NRS)
[151] Mar 8:34 (NRS)
[152] Isa 66:2 (NRS)

alienation is the choice of humankind and not a breach imposed by God as punishment. The pervasiveness of the alienation of humankind from God reaches its zenith in the generation of Noah.

> The LORD saw that the wickedness of humankind was great in the earth, and that every inclination of the thoughts of their hearts was only evil continually (כָל־יֵצֶר מַחְשְׁבֹת לִבּוֹ רַק רַע). And the LORD was sorry that he had made humankind on the earth, and it grieved him to his heart. So the LORD said, "I will blot out from the earth the human beings I have created-- people together with animals and creeping things and birds of the air, for I am sorry that I have made them." But Noah found favor in the sight of the LORD.[153]

In the generations after Cain, it had become the habitual choice of humankind to ignore the "Good" in favour of sin, or evil. This is no "infection" of sin or by sin. That it is "habitual" means that doing the "not-Good" has become a persistent choice. Yet if the sin were a part of the nature of humankind, repentance would not be possible.[154]

This observation by God of man's consistent behaviour is repeated after the flood when God had restored creation:

> And when the LORD smelled the pleasing odor, the LORD said in his heart, "I will never again curse the ground because of humankind, for the inclination of the human heart is evil from youth; nor will I ever again destroy every living creature as I have done.[155]

In this decision to make creation separate from Adam's malfeasances and no longer to punish the garden for the errors of the gardener, God notes that the human heart is misshapen and bent towards evil from youth. This is as close as the Bible ever

---

[153] Gen 6:5-8 (NRS)
[154] The likelihood is that this "evil" is, as with Cain, the sin of murder. Murder in the Bible is taking life without the permission of the life-giver. Since God gave Adam only fruit, vegetables and leafy things to eat in the beginning (Gen. 1:29-30), it is clear that no permission was given at first for taking the life of animals to eat their meat; to do so would be murder. Murder, then, was the evil that beset humankind in the generation of Noah. This probably included the murder of humans as well in warfare. Thus we see God giving the permissions for meat-eating at the end of the flood, though human murder is still prohibited (see Gen. 9:2-6).
[155] Gen 8:21 (NRS)

comes to talking about what in later Christian theology is deemed "original sin". It is different, however, from "original sin" in that choice still remains to Adam, it is still possible to choose "the Good", and there will be those humans who will be inclined towards "the Good" and righteousness (see Noah, below, for example). Again, repentance would not be possible if the inclination towards evil were absolute and unchangeable. In fact, repentance in Scripture is moving from an inclination to evil to the inclination towards good (בוטה רצי), often described as "behaving with righteousness"

While this idea of inclinations of the heart towards good or evil is normative from the earliest parables of Genesis, the development of the evil inclination by the time of the Dead Sea Scrolls and the time of Jesus is often towards a semi-personification of the "evil inclination" as the "evil one". However, it does not ever become a Devil or Satan and remains always a function of humankind itself.

> O inclination to evil, why were you formed to cover the land with deceit?[156]
> We must not be like Cain who was from the evil one and murdered his brother. And why did he murder him? Because his own deeds were evil and his brother's righteous.[157]
> And do not bring us to the time of trial, but rescue us from the evil one.[158]
> ...the field is the world, and the good seed are the children of the kingdom; the weeds are the children of the evil one,[159]
> But the Lord is faithful; he will strengthen you and guard you from the evil one.[160]

We must notice that God is more sad and grieved than he is angry by this choice of humankind to alienate himself from God by choosing evil. He regrets the human experiment he has made and would obliterate humanity and, in fact, all life from his creation in

---

[156] Sir 37:3 (NRS)
[157] 1Jo 3:12 (NRS)
[158] Mat 6:13 (NRS)
[159] Mat 13:38 (NRS)
[160] 2Th 3:3 (NRS)

frustration over human sin; but there is the tag to the inclination of God towards justice and his love of it. "But Noah found favour in the sight of the LORD." Further along we hear:

> Then the LORD said to Noah, "Go into the ark, you and all your household, for I have seen that you alone are righteous before me in this generation."[161]

Assertion 18: The concomitant major concern of Scripture is the reconciliation of that which is alienated. In a real sense, Noah's righteousness prevents God from allowing the total destruction of life, for to wipe out the righteous with the wicked would itself be unrighteous on God's part – and God will not behave unrighteously.[162] Therefore, God provides a tiny universe, the ark, to save the lives of Noah and his family, the repository of humanity, as well as the life of the animals in their breeding pairs. The righteousness of one man has saved humanity, or at least a microcosm of it. The alienation of humanity from God is not total and God embarks upon the process of the restoration of humankind. He does this by recruiting those who are righteous. The notion of a righteous remnant – or better, a righteous portion of humankind – underlies the principle of a "chosen people". Insight into the Divine Reasoning is given at the conclusion of the flood:

> Then Noah built an altar to the LORD, and took of every clean animal and of every clean bird, and offered burnt offerings on the altar. And when the LORD smelled the pleasing odor, the LORD said in his heart, "I will never again curse the ground because of humankind, for the inclination of the human heart is evil from youth; nor will I ever again destroy every living creature as I have done. As long as the earth endures, seedtime and harvest, cold and heat, summer and winter, day and night, shall not cease."[163]

---

[161] Gen 7:1 (NRS)
[162] "Far be it from you to do such a thing, to slay the righteous with the wicked, so that the righteous fare as the wicked! Far be that from you! Shall not the Judge of all the earth do what is just?" Gen 18:25 (NRS)
[163] Gen 8:20-22 (NRS)

Noah is "chosen" with his family for salvation from the flood because he is like-minded with God – "for I have seen that you alone are righteous before me in this generation." He is one who does "the good", as God suggested to Cain, the first son of man (Adam).

Noah's first act upon exiting the ark is to carry out the priestly function of sacrifice; and it is the smell of the sacrifice that moves the heart of God. We see several things in this sacrifice. First, that because the Lord accepts the sacrifice positively, we understand that God has changed his mind about the slaughter of animals, for there can be no sacrifice without the taking of animal life, heretofore reckoned as murder. Second, it is the smell of the sacrifice which is offered to God and which he accepts. This is undoubtedly the burning of the fat, and the fat portions are in the future that part of the animal, which are designated for the Lord in Israel's tradition.[164] Third, while there is no indication that this sacrifice has anything to do with sin, there is the clear indication that it has the effect of reconciliation. That God has sacrifice in mind from before the flood is indicated by his instructions to take seven pairs of clean animals (those that can be sacrificed) on the ark and only a single pair of the other animals.

In this new creation, for that is what it is, the priestly and sacrificial cult is to be at its heart. To attempt to read the Bible - the narrative of the reconciliation of that which is alienated from God by sin - without acknowledging the importance of the priestly, sacrificial cult, would be to miss the point of Scripture. Some have raised the objection of the anthropomorphic implications of God's enjoying the sweet smell of burning fat; such folks miss the parabolic nature of scripture's narrative, and perhaps need to go to a barbecue.

We are meant to understand that Noah emerges from the ark into a new creation. God is starting over with the enterprise, but this time

---

[164] There is not the slightest suggestion that God joins in the sacrifice or consumes any of it; it is just a nice smell which he enjoys.

he acknowledges the inevitability of man's taking animal life in order to eat meat and the ability to do so without committing the great sin of murder. Furthermore, he separates the durability of the creation from man's stewardship of it and in spite of man's follies.

> And when the LORD smelled the pleasing odor, the LORD said in his heart, "I will never again curse the ground because of humankind, for the inclination of the human heart is evil from youth; nor will I ever again destroy every living creature as I have done.[165]

This is an indulgence on God's part in the sense that the stability of creation is no longer endangered by human sin as regards the life of animals by eating meat, so long as the life is given back to the creator of it by dealing properly with the blood (called "making atonement" for the life of the animal which has been slaughtered). The taking of human life is still murder and always forbidden.[166]

Assertion 19: Because the Bible is parabolic narrative and not history, the notions of apocalyptic and eschatology are quite foreign to Scripture except in the short term. The Bible is concerned rather with the restoration of regularity and balance in the creation:

> As long as the earth endures, seedtime and harvest, cold and heat, summer and winter, day and night, shall not cease." God said, "This is the sign of the covenant that I make between me and you and every living creature that is with you, for all future generations: I have set my bow in the clouds, and it shall be a sign of the covenant between me and the earth. When I bring clouds over the earth and the bow is seen in the clouds, I will remember my covenant that is between me and you and every living creature of all flesh; and the waters shall never again become a flood to destroy all flesh. When the bow is in the clouds, I will see it and remember the everlasting covenant between God and every living creature of all flesh that is on the earth." God said to Noah, "This is the sign of the covenant that I have established between me and all flesh that is on the earth.[167]

---

[165] Gen 8:21 (NRS)
[166] I have dealt with the blood as life and the various kinds of sacrifice in my Jonah, the Reluctant Missionary, Gracewing: Leominster, p. 27, *ftn. 43*
[167] Gen 8:22 (NRS); Gen 9:12-17(NRS)

Once more, we are reminded that the Bible is about God and his creation, his dwelling. The covenant made here is primarily between God and the earth, and only derivatively with humankind and the other animals for which man is responsible. The notion that human history is of utmost importance to God is a conceit of humankind that the world was made for Adam rather than for God, who has no history. The destiny of humankind is not the concern of the Bible, though some have interpreted it that way. Nor is the Bible about the salvation of any individual or group of individuals. The universe is not going anywhere or evolving into anything else in Scripture.

Rather, the Bible gives us the vision of God for his creation and the instructions for keeping it that way. The vision is the same at the beginning and the end (the intent of "I am the Alpha and Omega.") This vision is always this-worldly and anticipates no other world or dimension. It is why Jews and Christians affirm the resurrection of the body (to this world made new) and not some spiritualisation to secure some otherworldly "heaven". If there is any eschatology in the Bible at all, it is only a looking forward to the re-ordering all things as they were in the beginning, especially at those times where alienation seems most intense:
> Since all these things are to be dissolved in this way, what sort of persons ought you to be in leading lives of holiness and godliness, waiting for and hastening the coming of the day of God, because of which the heavens will be set ablaze and dissolved, and the elements will melt with fire? But, in accordance with his promise, we wait for new heavens and a new earth, where righteousness is at home.[168]

The story of the rich young man who came to Jesus to inquire how he might win eternal life is again instructive:
> Then someone came to him and said, "Teacher, what good deed must I do to have eternal life?" And he said to him, "Why do you ask me about what is good? There is only one who is good. If you wish to enter into life, keep the commandments." He said to him, "Which ones?" And Jesus said, "You shall not murder;

---

[168] 2Pe 3:11-13 (NRS)

> You shall not commit adultery; You shall not steal; You shall not bear false witness; Honor your father and mother; also, You shall love your neighbor as yourself." The young man said to him, "I have kept all these; what do I still lack?" Jesus said to him, "If you wish to be perfect, go, sell your possessions, and give the money to the poor, and you will have treasure in heaven; then come, follow me." When the young man heard this word, he went away grieving, for he had many possessions.[169]

What Jesus is saying to this young man is that his goal is wrong; eternal life is not the point. The Ten Commandments were not given to provide a means of getting to "heaven". Rather, it is the accomplishment of the reconciliation of the world to God, which is the true goal: "Leave all other considerations behind and come, follow me in the work of reconciliation, the work of the kingdom." "Work for God's intentions and desires; everything else will be taken care of." This poor rich man cannot give up his own self-interest for the concerns of God; he wants to go to heaven and Jesus tells him heaven is not the goal. When the disciples object to this, Jesus replies:

> Jesus said to them, "Truly I tell you, at the renewal of all things, when the Son of Man is seated on the throne of his glory, you who have followed me will also sit on twelve thrones, judging the twelve tribes of Israel. And everyone who has left houses or brothers or sisters or father or mother or children or fields, for my name's sake, will receive a hundredfold, and will inherit eternal life. But many who are first will be last, and the last will be first.[170]

Note that here Jesus is clear that nothing else is the goal except "the renewal of all things (παλινγενεσία)." Only then will everything be sorted as to the rewards of the faithful.

Adam, following the flood, has still the function of serving in and watching over God's creation; but God has no destination or destiny, and neither does creation have a destiny, except to be

---

[169] Mat 19:16-22 (NRS)
[170] Mat 19:28-1(NRS)

restored to its primary state of goodness as the dwelling place of God.[171]

Alienation provides the only agenda of the biblical narrative, namely the restoration of the creation to God as his dwelling; and this agenda applies to humankind as a part of the creation. As we have seen, sin is a choice of man (starting with Cain), and sin causes alienation from the holiness of God. Since Adam was placed as the administrator and steward of the creation, which is the household of God, when Adam chooses to sin, he brings about the alienation of the whole creation from the God whose kingdom and dwelling place it is. Clearly, God wants his household back; all of it.[172]

Assertion 20: The story of the sacrifice of Noah makes it clear that the God of Scripture pays attention to and reacts to the intercession of the righteous when made on behalf of something or someone other than themselves. Whether Noah's intercession was compensatory for the lawlessness of the generation of the flood or, as is more likely, a re-purification of the earth after the flood is not entirely clear. That God is "soothed" by the smoke of the sacrifice and subsequently vows never to destroy the earth by flood again indicate his willingness to pay attention to the intercessions of certain human individuals who are "pure" by reason of their righteousness. Thus, we learn that a portion of humankind will be actively involved in the reconciliation of the world and the work of redemption of that which is alienated. As Adam in the beginning

---

[171] This is why John begins his Gospel with the story of creation and ends it with: And the one who was seated on the throne said, "See, I am making all things new." Also he said, "Write this, for these words are trustworthy and true." Then he said to me, "It is finished! I am the Alpha and the Omega, the beginning and the end. To the thirsty I will give water as a gift from the spring of the water of life." Rev 21:5-6 (NRS)

[172] Clearly, the Bible knows or cares nothing of the Hegelian process of history and evolution. Hebrew has only finished and unfinished modes of verbs. The life of the world in sin – "Every inclination of man's heart was evil continuously" – is unfinished. "All things made new" is finished, as it says: "Then he said to me, 'It is finished! I am the Alpha and the Omega, the beginning and the end.'" (Rev 21:6 NRS).

was placed in the garden to maintain its goodness, a son of Adam is now engaged in the work of restoring the goodness to creation.

Man will now take on the responsibility for the work of reconciling an alienated creation to the Creator. In Noah, God found one who was like-minded to himself, a righteous man who is responsive to God's intentions and through his agency takes the first steps in the work of reconciliation by offering a soothing odour to the Lord in the sacrifice he offers.

> Then God said to Noah and to his sons with him, "As for me, I am establishing my covenant with you and your descendants after you, and with every living creature that is with you, the birds, the domestic animals, and every animal of the earth with you, as many as came out of the ark. I establish my covenant with you, that never again shall all flesh be cut off by the waters of a flood, and never again shall there be a flood to destroy the earth."[173]

Assertion 21: Given the complete otherness of God from his creation, the God of the Bible acts in creation through the principle of Agency; his interventions are never direct. "Agent" may refer to one who acts for, or in the place of, another, by authority from him; one entrusted with the business of another. As we have seen the creation of Adam in the image and likeness of God intends to convey that Adam is the agent of God in creation, acting on God's behalf in the maintenance of God's household. In true agency, the one sent is equivalent to the one sending in power (in governmental agency, this is called "plenipotentiary") and authority. The Hebrew word "to send" (שָׁלַח) and the "one who is sent" (שָׁלִיחַ) are akin to the Greek ἀπόστολος, apostle. Of Adam, it says: "Therefore the LORD God *sent* him forth from the garden of Eden, to till the ground from which he was taken."[174]

After Noah, the task of Adam is no longer simply service, but more specifically service in the work of redeeming those who are

---

[173] Gen 9:8-11 (NRS)
[174] Gen 3:23 (NRS). The notion of service is closely related to the principle of agency, that is, the agent is the servant of the one sending.

alienated from God. The sacrifice of Noah is now the service, or the "divine service" (Greek, Λειτουργία) which seeks to reconcile God and his creation. Noah is the agent, then, who first represents God to his creation and represents creation to God through the priestly work of sacrifice, reconciling the world to God.

As we have noted above, the agent or servant of the God of the Bible must be like-minded with God, that is a person of righteousness and justice, choosing the Good. Further, the agent must be merciful, concerned with forgiveness and forswearing vengeance; and finally the agent must be humble, comfortable in the walk with God yet willing to take a second position in the relationship with God. In short, the agent must be holy as God is holy.

The servant is not self-appointed, but chosen (בָּחַר) by God. Being chosen is never being selected for special treatment or favouritism in Scripture. Rather, the servant is chosen for purpose and for function, and that purpose is always to do with the work of redemption and reconciliation. The temptation is, of course, that the chosen one or ones will come to believe in their election as establishing their importance according to the measures of the world. The declaration of Jesus on this subject reflects the Bible's standard judgment on this kind of arrogance:
> Bear fruits worthy of repentance. Do not begin to say to yourselves, 'We have Abraham as our ancestor'; for I tell you, God is able from these stones to raise up children to Abraham.[175]

Election in Scripture is not a permanent state or status; it is always contingent on the success of the one chosen to accomplish the goal given by God. God can elect and he can deselect:
> Then the LORD said, "Name him Lo-ammi, for you are not my people and I am not your God."[176] But later he says: And I will have pity on Lo-ruhamah, and I will say to Lo-ammi, "You are my people"; and he shall say, "You are my God."[177]

---
[175] Luk 3:8 (NRS)
[176] Hos 1:9 (NRS)
[177] Hos 2:23 (NRS)

Assertion 22: The principle of agency or election in the Bible raises the question of how the human agent is related to a God who is completely other to humankind.[178] Since there is never a consideration in Hebrew of "being" or "essence", the closest relationship we have biblically is that Adam, that is, all humans, are created in the image of God (בְּצַלְמֵנוּ כִּדְמוּתֵנוּ)[179]. This is a likeness of function or power, and it is in no sense identical. And since it belongs to everyman, another device is used by Scripture to describe the intimate relationship between the chosen and God.

In human terms, the closest relationship between two people is described as a "blood relationship" or a genetic association. But God is without blood or genes. The human relationship which must be permanent and intimate but which may never be genetic is, of course, the contract of marriage. The couple may not be related but must have a relationship that is as strong as a genetic one for the sake of the children. Since biblical marriage is a matter of contract, the Bible uses the contract of marriage to describe the relationship of God with those he has chosen. The contract must be freely chosen by both parties and its persistence depends upon absolute fidelity. The bride takes on the identity of the bridegroom but never becomes a part of the bridegroom. The contract of marriage defines most of the covenants that God makes with the chosen throughout the Bible. The icon of marriage as the description of the relationship between God and his chosen is most particularly connected with the Temple cult in Jerusalem and much of the imagery of that institution.

Another binding contract used by the Bible to describe the relationship between God and his chosen is that of adoption. Most

---

[178] The question of angels and angelology is at best secondary in Scripture. By the Bible's own understanding of God as Creator of everything, including angelic "messengers", these creatures, when mentioned at all, are always create and absolutely distinct from God. Their relationship with men is not really the Bible's concern. If the Bible mentions them at all, it is always (in good Hebrew fashion) in terms of a function; never in terms of "being" or "substance".
[179] Gen 1:26 (WTT)

world cultures accept adoption as creating an inseparable bond between two unrelated individuals as though it were a blood-bond, especially between father and son.[180] In Israel, all male children belong biologically to the mother (since there is never a question of "motherhood" for obvious reasons); the father adopts the son eight days later at the circumcision. By this adoption, the son is owned by the father's family, lineage and God, and the ownership is as permanent as a blood relationship. Such a device is most important in polygamous societies, as Israel's was.

The use of adoption as describing the relationship between God and his chosen one is more characteristic of the Wilderness Tradition and the northern Kingdom of Israel: "When Israel was a child, I loved him, and out of Egypt I called my son."[181] Again:
> I led them with cords of human kindness, with bands of love. I was to them like those who lift infants to their cheeks. I bent down to them and fed them.[182]
> Then you (Moses) shall say to Pharaoh, 'Thus says the LORD: Israel is my firstborn son. I said to you, "Let my son go that he may worship me." But you refused to let him go; now I will kill your firstborn son.'"[183]

The Bible does not speak of the "nature" of God or of the "nature" of the chosen, but only of their relationship as contract, of the purpose of the contract and the success or failure of the purpose of the contract, which is the reconciliation of the world.

Assertion 23: The iconic figure of the agent or servant of God in and throughout Scripture is Abraham. We know very little about him before his summons from God except that he comes out of that confusion of humankind that is signified by the Tower of Babel, or Babylon. Babylon is the Bible's description of man's

---

[180] Consider the case of the ancient Romans, for example, in which a child was not considered to belong to a family until the child, laid before the paterfamilias, was picked up by the father, and thus adopted, so to speak, by the father.
[181] Hos 11:1 (NRS)
[182] Hos 11:4 (NRS)
[183] Exo 4:22-23 (NRS)

own creation as the opposite of God's creation of his dwelling place, the heavens and the earth:
> And they said to one another, "Come, let us make bricks, and burn them thoroughly." And they had brick for stone, and bitumen for mortar. Then they said, "Come, let us build ourselves a city, and a tower with its top in the heavens, and let us make a name for ourselves; otherwise we shall be scattered abroad upon the face of the whole earth." The LORD came down to see the city and the tower, which mortals had built.[184]

The sin of Babylon is first of all the sin of human arrogance. "We shall be like God and create our own world." "Our name will be great as God's name is great." In fact, Babylon becomes the model of what is called "human civilisation" and the Bible puts forward here its basic distrust for human society and big cities. Primarily, cities are a place of the multiplicity of gods and idolatrous ideas. The gods are reflected by the hodgepodge of peoples that live in cities and their babel of tongues. Murder and license are the way of cities. The relativism required of many traditions existing side-by-side leads, in the Bible's judgment, to gross immoralities, a sort of *"Gott ist tot und alles ist gelaubt."*[185] This general prejudice against cities and civilisations is fairly standard throughout the Bible and accounts for the bias for the creativity of the wilderness as a place of formation and renewal. This penchant for the wilderness as normative should be born in mind in all biblical interpretation.[186]

As Noah was at the beginning of his narrative just another member of generation of the flood until God chose him by reason of his righteousness to a life of agency, so Abraham is described as just another member of the civilisation of the city.[187] There is not a record of Abraham's prior righteousness as there was with Noah. Yet God singled him out to be his agent in the world. The call is

---
[184] Gen 11:3-5 (NRS)
[185] F. Nietzsche, "God is dead and everything is allowed."
[186] When Israel later makes a distinction between themselves and the gentiles, the gentiles are these men of the Tower of Babel.
[187] It is possible that "Ur" of the Chaldeans is a form of "'Ir"(עיר) , or "City" of the Chaldeans, that is, Babylon. We might call it "the big city".

very terse: "Now the LORD said to Abram, 'Go...'".[188] "So Abram went, as the LORD had told him;"[189] Apparently it is the very willingness and action of Abraham to go that shows us his like-mindedness with God, his righteousness.

Clearly, Abraham has a choice. On the one hand, he can remain with his past and its securities and comforts. He is, after all, a man of great substance and wealth, and his wife is a princess (Sarai means princess). On the other hand, he can place his trust in this God whom he has just encountered for the first time and accept promises for the future, with no evidence that they can or will be made good by God. Because he chose the latter, the Bible says of him: "And he believed the LORD; and the LORD reckoned it to him as righteousness."[190] So, just as with Noah, God chooses one of like mind with himself, a righteous man, to become his agent. The purpose of the election of Abraham is clearly stated in the promise:
> I will make of you a great nation, and I will bless you, and make your name great, so that you will be a blessing. I will bless those who bless you, and the one who curses you I will curse; *and in you all the families of the earth shall be blessed*.[191]

Abraham, called from the nations – the Gentiles – will be the agent through whom God will redeem and restore the nations to himself. Abraham is the righteous remnant through whom God will redeem his world. Moreover, he is the forbearer of a specific people who are chosen to be "the Light to the Nations":
> I am the LORD, I have called you in righteousness, I have taken you by the hand and kept you; I have given you as a covenant to the people, a light to the nations, to open the eyes that are blind, to bring out the prisoners from the dungeon, from the prison those who sit in darkness.[192]

---

[188] Gen 12:1 (NRS)
[189] Gen 12:4 (NRS)
[190] Gen 15:6 (NRS)
[191] Gen 12:2-3 (NRS)
[192] Isa 42:6-7 (NRS)

Abraham is not a Jew or Judaean; he is rather one of the nations, a Gentile, whom God has chosen and to whom he has given the task of redemption of those who dwell in Babylon (that is, the nations of the world). Notice that his children after him are also to be righteous in order to carry on their task.[193] God associates himself with Abraham and his children and even names himself by them: "I am the God of your father, the God of Abraham, the God of Isaac, and the God of Jacob."[194]

Therefore, we see that God's choice of Abraham is not the choice of one man; it is the choice of a people (עַם), of whom Abraham is the progenitor and who arise from his generations, Isaac, Jacob and the twelve sons of Jacob. This people have distinction in the world by reason of the God who chose Abraham and thus also his generations, by the name by which their God calls them, by reason of the land which their God gives them, and – most especially – the task which Abraham's God gives to them:
> ...and your offspring shall be like the dust of the earth, and you shall spread abroad to the west and to the east and to the north and to the south; and all the families of the earth shall be blessed in you and in your offspring.[195]

The very personal nature of God's encounter with Abraham here and elsewhere in the narrative together with the free will, which this God allows humankind, reveals a compassionate God quite different from the "gods" of the nations. The God that Scripture presents negotiates rather than imposes his will. When God first makes a covenant with Abraham, it is God who deigns to obligate himself to the terms of the covenant:
> As the sun was going down, a deep sleep fell upon Abram, and a deep and terrifying darkness descended upon him. Then the LORD said to Abram, "Know this for certain, that your offspring

---

[193] It is useful here to remind ourselves that righteousness, like-mindedness with God, choseness and what we might call the "mind of the Messiah" are all related to each other. The righteous person has an inclination to do "the Good" which God first urged upon Cain.
[194] Exo 3:6 (NRS)
[195] Gen 28:14 (NRS)

> shall be aliens in a land that is not theirs, and shall be slaves there, and they shall be oppressed for four hundred years; but I will bring judgment on the nation that they serve, and afterward they shall come out with great possessions. As for yourself, you shall go to your ancestors in peace; you shall be buried in a good old age. And they shall come back here in the fourth generation; for the iniquity of the Amorites is not yet complete." When the sun had gone down and it was dark, a smoking fire pot and a flaming torch passed between these pieces. On that day the LORD made a covenant with Abram, saying, "To your descendants I give this land, from the river of Egypt to the great river, the river Euphrates;"[196]

When God is considering what to do about the cities of Sodom and Gomorrah, he chooses to discuss his decision with his friend Abraham and allows Abraham to argue with him about the disposition of these cities before he takes action:

> The LORD said, "Shall I hide from Abraham what I am about to do, seeing that Abraham shall become a great and mighty nation, and all the nations of the earth shall be blessed in him? No, for I have chosen him, that he may charge his children and his household after him to keep the way of the LORD by doing righteousness and justice; so that the LORD may bring about for Abraham what he has promised him." Then the LORD said, "How great is the outcry against Sodom and Gomorrah and how very grave their sin! I must go down and see whether they have done altogether according to the outcry that has come to me; and if not, I will know." So the men turned from there, and went toward Sodom, while Abraham remained standing before the LORD. Then Abraham came near and said, "Will you indeed sweep away the righteous with the wicked"?[197]

This familiarity with Abraham, his chosen one, puts us in mind of that original closeness between God and Adam when they used to walk together in the Garden in the cool of the day. Abraham even bargains and argues with God to save the cities of Sodom and Gomorrah, using God's own righteousness as a bargaining tool. Only Moses later has the courage to stand up to God and argue a

---

[196] Gen 15:12-18 (NRS)
[197] Gen 18:17-23 (NRS)

point of redemption, and this because God speaks with him as a friend, since Moses is "the most humble man on earth". [198]

Assertion 24: With the choosing of Abraham, the Bible undertakes two very different levels of concern and foci of attention, and the reader of the Bible must keep both in mind at all times. The first and most important, though often obscured by the second, is the continuing purpose of God in the reconciliation of the world to himself. We might call it the "Big Picture" and it is the overriding concern of the Bible. This is evident in the Bible's concern for the Gentiles and their repentance, conversion and restoration. As pointed out above, the very covenant with Abraham and his offspring has, as its stated purpose, the concern for the nations: "and all the families of the earth shall be blessed in you and in your offspring."[199] Clearly, Abraham and his seed are a means to this end and the reconciliation of all humankind to the Creator remains, throughout the Bible, the goal of God.

Yet we must also note that Abraham and his offspring are to be only <u>one</u> *means* of obtaining God's overarching goal. Their successes (or failures) are not ever to be confused with the "big picture", no matter who claims the promises of Abraham. That others can and are raised up as Chosen of the Lord to accomplish his greater purpose is shown by two particular passages of Scripture. Consider the occasion of the choosing of those who were to share the spirit of Moses in leading the people:
> Then the LORD came down in the cloud and spoke to him, and took some of the spirit that was on him and put it on the seventy elders; and when the spirit rested upon them, they prophesied. But they did not do so again. Two men remained in the camp, one named Eldad, and the other named Medad, and the spirit rested on them; they were among those registered, but they had not gone out to the tent, and so they prophesied in the camp. And a young man ran and told Moses, "Eldad and Medad are prophesying in the camp." And Joshua son of Nun, the assistant of Moses, one of his chosen men, said, "My lord Moses, stop

---
[198] Num 12:3-8 (NRS)
[199] Gen 28:14 (NRS)

> them!" But Moses said to him, "Are you jealous for my sake? Would that all the LORD's people were prophets, and that the LORD would put his spirit on them!" And Moses and the elders of Israel returned to the camp.[200]

God always retains the right of appointment of his agents, no matter their pedigree. Even more dramatic is God's designation of a messiah well apart from the offspring of Abraham:

> Thus says the LORD to his anointed, to Cyrus, whose right hand I have grasped to subdue nations before him and strip kings of their robes, to open doors before him-- and the gates shall not be closed:[201]

These reminders of God's larger purposes even appear in the Passover narratives before the establishment of Israel in its land:

> For the LORD your God is God of gods and Lord of lords, the great God, mighty and awesome, who is not partial and takes no bribe, who executes justice for the orphan and the widow, and who loves the strangers, providing them food and clothing. *You shall also love the stranger*, for you were strangers in the land of Egypt.[202]
>
> ...there shall be one law for the native and *for the alien* who resides among you.[203]
>
> As for the assembly, there shall be for both you and the resident alien a single statute, a perpetual statute throughout your generations; *you and the alien shall be alike before the LORD*. You and the alien who resides with you shall have the same law and the same ordinance.[204]

As the narrative of Israel as a specific people intensifies throughout the course of the Exodus from Egypt and the wandering in the wilderness, the vision of God concerning the nations gives way to the daily events of Israel's own story. The nation of Egypt becomes the oppressor rather than the concern of God's redemption.[205] When Israel enters the land, the narrative is almost

---

[200] Num 11:25-30 (NRS)
[201] Isa 45:1 (NRS)
[202] Deu 10:17-19 (NRS)
[203] Exo 12:49 (NRS)
[204] Num 15:15-16 (NRS)
[205] Though the later rabbis tell a story which returns to the notion of God's concern for all peoples in The Talmud Babli, (Megillah 10b).

exclusively about the wars against the peoples who are displaced by Israel's invasion. These wars against the "enemy" nations continue throughout the time of the judges and intensify with the coming of the kings. There is a significant eclipse of the "Big Picture" of God's intent to redeem humankind from Solomon until the end of the monarchies; the safety of the people of Israel becomes paramount, with the possible exception of a few of the prophets of the later kingdoms who keep God's concerns before the king and people.

If there is an effort towards extra-national mission, it is through assimilation, on the principle laid down in Exodus concerning aliens and the Passover:
> If an alien who resides with you wants to celebrate the passover to the LORD, all his males shall be circumcised; then he may draw near to celebrate it; he shall be regarded as a native of the land. But no uncircumcised person shall eat of it;[206]
> It (the Passover) was eaten by the people of Israel who had returned from exile, and also by all who had joined them and separated themselves from the pollutions of the nations of the land to worship the LORD, the God of Israel.[207]

This policy of Assimilationism was, of course, the practise of the earliest Christian Church in obtaining converts; the gentile had first to become a Jew and then a Christian.

With the destruction of the national identity of the northern Kingdom of Israel by the Assyrians we begin to see a glimmer of the return to God's concern for the redemption of the nations, especially in the Book of Jonah.[208] Not until the destruction of Jerusalem and its Temple by the Babylonians does the thinking of the Judaeans begin to move from Jerusalem as a national bastion and the Temple as a strictly national fortress to a world-centre for attracting the nations of the world to the Lord God. Much of this

---

[206] Exo 12:48 (NRS)
[207] Ezr 6:21 (NRS)
[208] I have explored this return to the universalism in biblical thought in my, Jonah, the Reluctant Missionary, op. cit.

has to do with the removal of the kings of Judah so that the real King can become evident, even God himself.[209] As it says in Zechariah the Prophet: "And the LORD will become king over all the earth; on that day the LORD will be one and his name one."[210] The kings, which were after all an indulgence on God's part, had become an impediment to the larger world purpose of God, and their demise allows once again the shining forth of the Lord's real purposes for his creation.

Jerusalem will now become a centre for the Lord's appearing and the gathering of peoples in his presence, but it will become one that attracts rather than repels the peoples of the world:

> Many peoples and strong nations shall come to seek the LORD of hosts in Jerusalem, and to entreat the favor of the LORD. Thus says the LORD of hosts: In those days ten men from nations of every language shall take hold of a Jew, grasping his garment and saying, "Let us go with you, for we have heard that God is with you."[211]
>
> Arise, shine; for your light has come, and the glory of the LORD has risen upon you. For darkness shall cover the earth, and thick darkness the peoples; but the LORD will arise upon you, and his

---

[209] The Book of Job is perhaps the reflection on the destruction of Jerusalem and its nationalistic obsessions to the greater plan of God for the nations. Careful attention needs to be paid to the passage in Job:

> After the LORD had spoken these words to Job, the LORD said to Eliphaz the Temanite: "My wrath is kindled against you and against your two friends; for you have not spoken of me what is right, as my servant Job has. Now therefore take seven bulls and seven rams, and go to my servant Job, and *offer up for yourselves a burnt offering; and my servant Job shall pray for you, for I will accept his prayer* not to deal with you according to your folly; for you have not spoken of me what is right, as my servant Job has done." So Eliphaz the Temanite and Bildad the Shuhite and Zophar the Naamathite went and did what the LORD had told them; and the LORD accepted Job's prayer. And the LORD restored the fortunes of Job when he had prayed for his friends; and the LORD gave Job twice as much as he had before. Job 42:7-10 (NRS). The reward for Job's sufferings is the salvation of his three friends (the three wise men from the east, the gentiles, who appear again at the Christian Epiphany).

[210] Zec 14:9 (NRS)
[211] Zec 8:22-23 (NRS

> glory will appear over you. Nations shall come to your light, and kings to the brightness of your dawn.[212]
>
> Many nations shall join themselves to the LORD on that day, and shall be my people; and I will dwell in your midst. And you shall know that the LORD of hosts has sent me to you. The LORD will inherit Judah as his portion in the holy land, and will again choose Jerusalem. Be silent, all people, before the LORD; for he has roused himself from his holy dwelling.[213]
>
> For I know their works and their thoughts, and I am coming to gather all nations and tongues; and they shall come and shall see my glory, and I will set a sign among them. From them I will send survivors to the nations, to Tarshish, Put, and Lud-- which draw the bow-- to Tubal and Javan, to the coastlands far away that have not heard of my fame or seen my glory; and they shall declare my glory among the nations. They shall bring all your kindred from all the nations as an offering to the LORD, on horses, and in chariots, and in litters, and on mules, and on dromedaries, to my holy mountain Jerusalem, says the LORD, just as the Israelites bring a grain offering in a clean vessel to the house of the LORD. And I will also take some of them as priests and as Levites, says the LORD. For as the new heavens and the new earth, which I will make, shall remain before me, says the LORD; so shall your descendants and your name remain.[214]

A second focus of our attention in biblical study that occurs with the call of Abraham is the beginning of the narrative of the particular chosen people of Israel. This narrative, in its particularism, often overwhelms the larger purpose of God for the reconciliation of the world to himself. The servant people from time to time and from their own perspective move to centre-stage as the real subjects and primary actors of the narrative. This is particularly true in the time of the kings and their wars, when winning battles becomes the goal. Mission for God is traded for self-perpetuation and even self-aggrandisement. The temptation of the reader is to be caught up in these affairs of the "Chosen" while forgetting the "Big Picture" of reconciling the world to the Creator

---

[212] Isa 60:1-3 (NRS)
[213] Zec 2:11-13 (NRS)
[214] Isa 66:18-22 (NRS)

described above. Status overrides function and purpose in the understanding of choseness.[215]

Jesus reminds us of this point, when he says:
> Not everyone who says to me, 'Lord, Lord,' will enter the kingdom of heaven, but only the one who does the will of my Father in heaven.[216] And again:
>
> They answered him, "Abraham is our father." Jesus said to them, "If you were Abraham's children, you would be doing what Abraham did.[217] And also:
>
> Bear fruits worthy of repentance. Do not begin to say to yourselves, 'We have Abraham as our ancestor'; for I tell you, God is able from these stones to raise up children to Abraham.[218]

The temptation to treat the Bible as history only makes the narrative of Israel's doings even more attractive, as the stories of long-ago heroes and villains are quite entertaining, especially since they have little attachment to the present. This arises from the attempt to find meaning in Scripture rather than purpose, as described in Assertion 1. We are tempted to ask from the biblical narrative, "Is Israel winning or losing here?" rather than "Is God's purpose being accomplished?" When the Church pretends to supplant Israel in the status of "Choseness", we find this triumphalism in such musical expressions as "Onward! Christian Soldiers". Servanthood for God is supplanted by self-service, self-congratulation and an incredible arrogance. As Joshua said to the people so eloquently:
> And if it seem evil unto you to serve the LORD, choose you this day whom ye will serve; whether the gods which your fathers served that were beyond the River, or the gods of the Amorites,

---

[215] The reminder about real purpose is often to be found in the mouths of the prophets. It is one of the paramount preachments of Jesus in the New Testament, though the Church later often becomes obsessed with its own self-perpetuation and success. We are reminded of the principle of architecture that form is to follow function and not the other way around!
[216] Mat 7:21 (NRS)
[217] Joh 8:39 (NRS)
[218] Luk 3:8 (NRS)

in whose land ye dwell; but as for me and my house, we will serve the LORD.'[219]

Assertion 25: While the call of Abraham and his offspring, the patriarchs, is the election of a people, the call of Moses represents the ordering and activation of this people for the purposes of God in the work of redemption. The people are lying in morbidity in the tomb which is Egypt; held by the power of death as is signified by Pharaoh, the god-king of Egypt; ignorant of their own God; and alien in a land which is not theirs. Their work there is to serve Pharaoh and contribute to the glory of Egypt and Egypt's god.[220] They are surrounded by a culture which glorifies death and which spends most of the life of this world preparing for and sustaining those who have entered into the after-life. Moses is confronted by the God of Life and commissioned to raise the people of Israel from their grave, to order them and to return them to the God who will restore them to his own place of life, the Land of Promise. The continuity of this people with their progenitors is rehearsed in the Psalm:

> Remember the wonderful works he has done, his miracles, and the judgments he uttered, O offspring of his servant Abraham, children of Jacob, his chosen ones. He is the LORD our God; his judgments are in all the earth. He is mindful of his covenant forever, of the word that he commanded, for a thousand generations, the covenant that he made with Abraham, his sworn promise to Isaac, which he confirmed to Jacob as a statute, to Israel as an everlasting covenant, saying, "To you I will give the land of Canaan as your portion for an inheritance." When they were few in number, of little account, and strangers in it, wandering from nation to nation, from one kingdom to another people, he allowed no one to oppress them; he rebuked kings on their account, saying, "Do not touch my anointed ones; do my prophets no harm."[221]

---

[219] Jos 24:15 (JPS)
[220] Egypt is more or less a consistent consideration in biblical studies from Abraham to the destruction of the Temple in 70 CE.
[221] Psa 105:5-15 (NRS)

As we have noted, their election is purposeful and never to be self-serving or self-aggrandising, for it is based not on their merit, but on their election by God:

> For you are a people holy to the LORD your God; the LORD your God has chosen you out of all the peoples on earth to be his people, his treasured possession. It was not because you were more numerous than any other people that the LORD set his heart on you and chose you-- for you were the fewest of all peoples. It was because the LORD loved you and kept the oath that he swore to your ancestors, that the LORD has brought you out with a mighty hand, and redeemed you from the house of slavery, from the hand of Pharaoh king of Egypt. Know therefore that the LORD your God is God, the faithful God who maintains covenant loyalty with those who love him and keep his commandments, to a thousand generations;[222]

The goal and purpose of this people is:

> I am the LORD, I have called you in righteousness, I have taken you by the hand and kept you; I have given you as a covenant to the people, a light to the nations, to open the eyes that are blind, to bring out the prisoners from the dungeon, from the prison those who sit in darkness.[223]

Psalm 105:15 quoted above: "Do not touch my anointed ones; do my prophets no harm" raises another interesting point for this work. The Psalm is clearly a hymn about the patriarchs from Abraham to Jacob, but before moving to Joseph, the descent into Egypt and the rise of Moses and Aaron, it inserts the present verse. This suggests that the patriarchs were prophets, but most importantly that they were reckoned to be "anointed ones" – messiahs (Hebrew uses בִּמְשִׁיחָי in the plural!). Now Abraham is called a prophet with the power of intercession in the case of Abimelech in Genesis 20:7, but this reference to the patriarchs as messiahs is unique. Clearly, the patriarchs were not kings; therefore, we shall have to look elsewhere for the significance of "messiah". Since there seems to be no indication that oil was poured on them, anointing must be something that God does, even

---

[222] Deu 7:6-9 (NRS)
[223] Isa 42:6-7 (NRS)

in the absence of oil. There is also the implication that those who arise from the patriarchs, namely the people of Israel, are a messianic people, chosen and set apart by God for his special purpose. Clearly, this is the designation of the people as infused by the spirit of God, as Ezekiel describes it:

> I will give them one heart, and put a new spirit within them; I will remove the heart of stone from their flesh and give them a heart of flesh, so that they may follow my statutes and keep my ordinances and obey them. Then they shall be my people, and I will be their God.[224]

While the narrative of this people is lengthy and consumes the better part of the Bible, the formation of the people begins at the Re(e)d Sea and occupies the entire wilderness tradition until the people are birthed at the crossing of the Jordan into the Land of Promise. The wilderness is the womb of Israel during which are formed all the major institutions that characterise the later life in the Land. The wilderness tradition is the touchstone for all Israel's later development and it is the place where re-formation takes place. The wilderness can be likened to the formless, aimless and darkling void out of which God called the very creation in the beginning.

The study of Scripture requires that Israel's narrative later be measured, not by the era of kings or the accounts of the Babylonian Exile, but by the formation of the wilderness. The emergence of the kings, the governors and princes, even the judges are derivative in some way from the surrounding nations and are not part of the wilderness formation. There is, however, no understanding of the people of Israel without an intimate knowledge of the place and conditions of their formation in the beginning, in the wilderness.

Assertion 26: There is nothing evolutionary about the "history" of Israel. It is a major and misleading error to assume, as the German Protestant biblical scholars did, that Israel's story begins

---

[224] Eze 11:19-20 (NRS)

with the primitive and moves to the sophisticated and more highly developed time of the Babylonian Exile. The assumption that the people of Moses' day could neither read nor write and that the stories of the Exodus were a much later account read back into the record totally ignores the highly developed culture of the Egypt from which Israel came and where Israel had lived for many years. This is not an account of ignorant nomads. Their "slavery" in Egypt does not mean that no one of them had any education or learning and that they were in some way coarse and unlettered, since all the peoples of Egypt were in fact indentured "slaves" of Pharaoh.

In short, the rich narrative of the Exodus needs to be accepted for what it is: a self-reflective narrative and liturgy of the time and of the actual experience of Israel's beginnings in the wilderness. The recitation of this narrative brings the reality of the Exodus into every present time and place. Furthermore, there is nothing remotely romantic or epic about the wilderness event. The wilderness was for Israel a time of fear, extreme discomfort and often wretchedness for the people. Their complaints were constant; many wished to turn back and be quit of the experience. It certainly was not a rational or sensible experience; it is truly God's idea and purpose. For it would not have been Israel's choice.

The real value of the wilderness is that there is nothing there and it is truly a "no-man's land". God chooses it precisely because it is a void. It is in the wilderness that the people are reduced to total neediness and an inability to save or support themselves. There is no available food or water, no pastureland, no buildings or niceties of civilisation. Israel meets its God from a position of utter helplessness and dependence:
> When Israel was a child, I loved him, and out of Egypt I called my son. ... Yet it was I who taught Ephraim to walk, I took them up in my arms; but they did not know that I healed them. I led them with cords of human kindness, with bands of love. I

was to them like those who lift infants to their cheeks. I bent down to them and fed them.[225]

So pervasive is the experience of the wilderness in the later experience of Israel that the scriptural account from the crossing of the Jordan onwards is nearly always retrospective in some way of the wilderness experience, and the major institutions of the wilderness are the norm for Israel's later experiences and life. The almost creedal formulation at the presentation of offerings to the Lord at the Feast of First Fruits even after the occupation of the Promised Land suggests that the wilderness is to be forever the touchstone of Israel's later life.[226]

The only exceptions to this constant referring back to the wilderness as the "good old days" are those experiences borrowed from the peoples of the land in which Israel finds itself after the Jordan crossing. Exceptions to a reliance on the norm of the wilderness are particularly true of the monarchies, which are both foreign to Israel's experience and derivative from other cultures and religions. Anything that is not from the wilderness is treated by scripture as suspicious in terms of authenticity.

This is certainly not to say that the wilderness traditions do not undergo modifications of time and event; it simply holds that post-wilderness experiences look backward to the wilderness for their authenticity. The need for constant renewal by accessing the wilderness tradition is declared by Moses before his death and the entry of the people into the Promised Land:
> Remember the days of old, consider the years long past; ask your father, and he will inform you; your elders, and they will tell you. When the Most High apportioned the nations, when he divided humankind, he fixed the boundaries of the peoples according to the number of the gods; the LORD's own portion was his people, Jacob his allotted share. He sustained him in a desert land, in a howling wilderness waste; he shielded him, cared for him, guarded him as the apple of his eye. As an eagle

---
[225] Hos 11:1, 3-4 (NRS)
[226] Cf. Deu. 32 below.

> stirs up its nest, and hovers over its young; as it spreads its wings, takes them up, and bears them aloft on its pinions, the LORD alone guided him; no foreign god was with him. He set him atop the heights of the land, and fed him with produce of the field; he nursed him with honey from the crags, with oil from flinty rock; curds from the herd, and milk from the flock, with fat of lambs and rams; Bashan bulls and goats, together with the choicest wheat-- you drank fine wine from the blood of grapes. Jacob ate his fill; Jeshurun grew fat, and kicked.
> Moses came and recited all the words of this song in the hearing of the people, he and Joshua son of Nun. When Moses had finished reciting all these words to all Israel, he said to them: "Take to heart all the words that I am giving in witness against you today; give them as a command to your children, so that they may diligently observe all the words of this law. This is no trifling matter for you, but rather your very life; through it you may live long in the land that you are crossing over the Jordan to possess."[227]

And again:
> When you have come into the land that the LORD your God is giving you as an inheritance to possess, and you possess it, and settle in it, you shall take some of the first of all the fruit of the ground, which you harvest from the land that the LORD your God is giving you, and you shall put it in a basket and go to the place that the LORD your God will choose as a dwelling for his name. You shall go to the priest who is in office at that time, and say to him, "Today I declare to the LORD your God that I have come into the land that the LORD swore to our ancestors to give us." When the priest takes the basket from your hand and sets it down before the altar of the LORD your God, you shall make this response before the LORD your God: "<u>A wandering Aramean was my ancestor</u>; he went down into Egypt and lived there as an alien, few in number, and there he became a great nation, mighty and populous. When the Egyptians treated us harshly and afflicted us, by imposing hard labor on us, we cried to the LORD, the God of our ancestors; the LORD heard our voice and saw our affliction, our toil, and our oppression. The LORD brought us out of Egypt with a mighty hand and an outstretched arm, with a terrifying display of power, and with

---

[227] Deu 32:7-15, 44-47 (NRS)

signs and wonders; and he brought us into this place and gave us this land, a land flowing with milk and honey. So now I bring the first of the fruit of the ground that you, O LORD, have given me." You shall set it down before the LORD your God and bow down before the LORD your God.[228]

Even if you are exiled to the ends of the world, from there the LORD your God will gather you, and from there he will bring you back. The LORD your God will bring you into the land that your ancestors possessed, and you will possess it; he will make you more prosperous and numerous than your ancestors. Moreover, the LORD your God will circumcise your heart and the heart of your descendants, so that you will love the LORD your God with all your heart and with all your soul, in order that you may live.[229]

Remember the long way that the LORD your God has led you these forty years in the wilderness, in order to humble you, testing you to know what was in your heart, whether or not you would keep his commandments. He humbled you by letting you hunger, then by feeding you with manna, with which neither you nor your ancestors were acquainted, in order to make you understand that one does not live by bread alone, but by every word that comes from the mouth of the LORD. The clothes on your back did not wear out and your feet did not swell these forty years. Know then in your heart that as a parent disciplines a child so the LORD your God disciplines you. Therefore keep the commandments of the LORD your God, by walking in his ways and by fearing him. For the LORD your God is bringing you into a good land, a land with flowing streams, with springs and underground waters welling up in valleys and hills, a land of wheat and barley, of vines and fig trees and pomegranates, a land of olive trees and honey, a land where you may eat bread without scarcity, where you will lack nothing, a land whose stones are iron and from whose hills you may mine copper. You shall eat your fill and bless the LORD your God for the good land that he has given you. Take care that you do not forget the LORD your God, by failing to keep his commandments, his ordinances, and his statutes, which I am commanding you today. When you have eaten your fill and have built fine houses and live in them, and

---

[228] Deu 26:1-10 (NRS)
[229] Deu 30:4-6 (NRS)

stirs up its nest, and hovers over its young; as it spreads its wings, takes them up, and bears them aloft on its pinions, the LORD alone guided him; no foreign god was with him. He set him atop the heights of the land, and fed him with produce of the field; he nursed him with honey from the crags, with oil from flinty rock; curds from the herd, and milk from the flock, with fat of lambs and rams; Bashan bulls and goats, together with the choicest wheat-- you drank fine wine from the blood of grapes. Jacob ate his fill; Jeshurun grew fat, and kicked.

Moses came and recited all the words of this song in the hearing of the people, he and Joshua son of Nun. When Moses had finished reciting all these words to all Israel, he said to them: "Take to heart all the words that I am giving in witness against you today; give them as a command to your children, so that they may diligently observe all the words of this law. This is no trifling matter for you, but rather your very life; through it you may live long in the land that you are crossing over the Jordan to possess."[227]

And again:

When you have come into the land that the LORD your God is giving you as an inheritance to possess, and you possess it, and settle in it, you shall take some of the first of all the fruit of the ground, which you harvest from the land that the LORD your God is giving you, and you shall put it in a basket and go to the place that the LORD your God will choose as a dwelling for his name. You shall go to the priest who is in office at that time, and say to him, "Today I declare to the LORD your God that I have come into the land that the LORD swore to our ancestors to give us." When the priest takes the basket from your hand and sets it down before the altar of the LORD your God, you shall make this response before the LORD your God: "<u>A wandering Aramean was my ancestor</u>; he went down into Egypt and lived there as an alien, few in number, and there he became a great nation, mighty and populous. When the Egyptians treated us harshly and afflicted us, by imposing hard labor on us, we cried to the LORD, the God of our ancestors; the LORD heard our voice and saw our affliction, our toil, and our oppression. The LORD brought us out of Egypt with a mighty hand and an outstretched arm, with a terrifying display of power, and with

---

[227] Deu 32:7-15, 44-47 (NRS)

signs and wonders; and he brought us into this place and gave us this land, a land flowing with milk and honey. So now I bring the first of the fruit of the ground that you, O LORD, have given me." You shall set it down before the LORD your God and bow down before the LORD your God.[228]

Even if you are exiled to the ends of the world, from there the LORD your God will gather you, and from there he will bring you back. The LORD your God will bring you into the land that your ancestors possessed, and you will possess it; he will make you more prosperous and numerous than your ancestors. Moreover, the LORD your God will circumcise your heart and the heart of your descendants, so that you will love the LORD your God with all your heart and with all your soul, in order that you may live.[229]

Remember the long way that the LORD your God has led you these forty years in the wilderness, in order to humble you, testing you to know what was in your heart, whether or not you would keep his commandments. He humbled you by letting you hunger, then by feeding you with manna, with which neither you nor your ancestors were acquainted, in order to make you understand that one does not live by bread alone, but by every word that comes from the mouth of the LORD. The clothes on your back did not wear out and your feet did not swell these forty years. Know then in your heart that as a parent disciplines a child so the LORD your God disciplines you. Therefore keep the commandments of the LORD your God, by walking in his ways and by fearing him. For the LORD your God is bringing you into a good land, a land with flowing streams, with springs and underground waters welling up in valleys and hills, a land of wheat and barley, of vines and fig trees and pomegranates, a land of olive trees and honey, a land where you may eat bread without scarcity, where you will lack nothing, a land whose stones are iron and from whose hills you may mine copper. You shall eat your fill and bless the LORD your God for the good land that he has given you. Take care that you do not forget the LORD your God, by failing to keep his commandments, his ordinances, and his statutes, which I am commanding you today. When you have eaten your fill and have built fine houses and live in them, and

---

[228] Deu 26:1-10 (NRS)
[229] Deu 30:4-6 (NRS)

> when your herds and flocks have multiplied, and your silver and gold is multiplied, and all that you have is multiplied, then do not exalt yourself, forgetting the LORD your God, who brought you out of the land of Egypt, out of the house of slavery, who led you through the great and terrible wilderness, an arid wasteland with poisonous snakes and scorpions. He made water flow for you from flint rock, and fed you in the wilderness with manna that your ancestors did not know, to humble you and to test you, and in the end to do you good. Do not say to yourself, "My power and the might of my own hand have gotten me this wealth." But remember the LORD your God, for it is he who gives you power to get wealth, so that he may confirm his covenant that he swore to your ancestors, as he is doing today.[230]

This narrative of the wilderness becomes, of course, the Haggadah of the Passover Feast and entails the recounting of the entire wilderness experience from the going out from Egypt until the coming into the land:
> You shall tell your child on that day, 'It is because of what the LORD did for me when I came out of Egypt.' It shall serve for you as a sign on your hand and as a reminder on your forehead, so that the teaching of the LORD may be on your lips; for with a strong hand the LORD brought you out of Egypt.[231]

One verse quoted above gives us a sense of the complete and childlike simplicity of the wilderness experience:
> He humbled you by letting you hunger, then by feeding you with manna, with which neither you nor your ancestors were acquainted, in order to make you understand that one does not live by bread alone, but by every word that comes from the mouth of the LORD. The clothes on your back did not wear out and your feet did not swell these forty years. Know then in your heart that as a parent disciplines a child so the LORD your God disciplines you.[232]

This kind of simplicity is the true "faith" of Scripture suggesting basic and total dependence upon deity for food and drink. Here, too, is the real mystery of the Sabbath, where resting suggests no

---

[230] Deu 8:2-18 (NRS)
[231] Exo 13:8-9 (NRS)
[232] Deu 8:3-5 (NRS)

self-dependence, only radical God-reliance.[233] We are also reminded here that true humility is to become child-like in our dependence and is the foundation of Israel's religion, first acquired in the wilderness.

We shall see elsewhere that the wilderness lies at the heart of Jesus' teaching in the New Testament. This is displayed in Jesus' teaching about the Kingdom and children:
> He called a child, whom he put among them, and said, "Truly I tell you, unless you change and become like children, you will never enter the kingdom of heaven. Whoever becomes humble like this child is the greatest in the kingdom of heaven.[234]

For Jesus, the child is not innocent but dependent upon parents and others for its very life and welfare. And so he teaches that unless someone becomes dependent upon God as a child upon its parent, this person cannot be a part of the Kingdom. Again, humility is for Jesus the foundation of the religion of Israel first learned in the wilderness. In like manner, Jesus speaks so often of the "little ones", the "poor", "the dependents" in society simply because they are, like the child, dependent ultimately upon God as father. He lists such humble folk in the Beatitudes in Matthew 5.

Assertion 27: There is a noteworthy difference between Scripture and our modern understanding when it comes to what is meant by reality and our perception of what is real. We have spoken earlier about the uniqueness of the Semitic languages (and the Greek derived from the Semitic mind-set) in its preference for verbs over nouns. Actions speak louder than things in Scripture, and because of this, reality will be perceived in the action rather than the static object or idea. We moderns, convinced of the truth of science, have a particularly difficult time with the Bible's view of the world and of God.

---

[233] We remember that Israel was not permitted to gather manna on the Sabbath, but a double portion on the Friday.
[234] Mat 18:2-4 (NRS)

We like to speak of the realities of science as tangible, measureable, quantifiable and substantial. Like St. Thomas, we maintain: "Unless I see the mark of the nails in his hands, and put my finger in the mark of the nails and my hand in his side, I will not believe."[235] In short, the resurrection is not real without scientific verification.

We can see the difference in the biblical text itself. Jesus tells the parable of the Sower Going Forth to Sow:
> "Listen! A sower went out to sow. And as he sowed, some seed fell on the path, and the birds came and ate it up. Other seed fell on rocky ground, where it did not have much soil, and it sprang up quickly, since it had no depth of soil. And when the sun rose, it was scorched; and since it had no root, it withered away. Other seed fell among thorns, and the thorns grew up and choked it, and it yielded no grain. Other seed fell into good soil and brought forth grain, growing up and increasing and yielding thirty and sixty and a hundredfold."[236]

The intention of the parable is, as always, reflected in the verb – the action of sowing seeds as a farmer does. The issue is whether or not the farmer should sow the seed (in this case, proclaim the Gospel) just because some of it will fall in places where it will not grow. The answer is that his task is to sow lavishly and extravagantly, no matter where the seed falls, for the seed that falls in good soil will yield many times over what might be wasted. In short, proclaim the Gospel with no thought about the effect, for God will take care of it from there.

Now some later Christian community not being comfortable with parables has sought to give it an interpretation which ignores the verb and looks for reality in the nouns in the narrative:
> When he was alone, those who were around him along with the twelve asked him about the parables.[237] And he said to them,

---

[235] Joh 20:25 (NRS)
[236] Mar 4:3-8 (NRS)
[237] Note that it is not the Twelve who interpret this way, but others. I would guess that they are the Petrine Christians in Rome for whom Mark writes. It is likely that this section is a homiletic gloss on Mark's text. There is also an almost gnostic (secret

"To you has been given the secret of the kingdom of God, but for those outside, everything comes in parables; in order that 'they may indeed look, but not perceive, and may indeed listen, but not understand; so that they may not turn again and be forgiven.'" And he said to them, "Do you not understand this parable? Then how will you understand all the parables? The sower sows the word. These are the ones on the path where the word is sown: when they hear, Satan immediately comes and takes away the word that is sown in them. And these are the ones sown on rocky ground: when they hear the word, they immediately receive it with joy. But they have no root, and endure only for a while; then, when trouble or persecution arises on account of the word, immediately they fall away. And others are those sown among the thorns: these are the ones who hear the word, but the cares of the world, and the lure of wealth, and the desire for other things come in and choke the word, and it yields nothing. And these are the ones sown on the good soil: they hear the word and accept it and bear fruit, thirty and sixty and a hundredfold."[238]

The parable of Jesus has now turned into an allegory, where meaning is no longer attached to the verb but to the nouns. The understanding of reality has also changed in the interpretation of things rather than actions. We moderns might find it more satisfying as it uses our own inclinations for the identification of what is real; but it misrepresents Jesus' own understanding of reality.

Another feature of Israel's religion which is significant in understanding the Bible's view of reality is its understanding and appreciation of "Speaking" and "Naming". This has been discussed often in terms of the power of the "Word" as we find in the Prologue of John's Gospel: "In the beginning was the Word, and the Word was with God, and the Word was God; Ἐν ἀρχῇ ἦν ὁ λόγος, καὶ ὁ λόγος ἦν πρὸς τὸν θεόν, καὶ θεὸς ἦν ὁ λόγος."[239] This Word becomes reality by being spoken: "And the Word became

---

knowledge reserved for "insiders") flavour to this as is characteristic of the gnostic Gospel of Thomas.
[238] Mar 4:10-20 (NRS)
[239] Joh 1:1 (NRS) and (BGT)

flesh (read, Reality) and lived among us; Καὶ ὁ λόγος σὰρξ ἐγένετοκαὶ καὶ ἐσκήνωσεν ἐν ἡμῖν"[240].

John's Prologue, however, is simply a re-statement in Greek of the Creation narrative in Genesis which is in Hebrew. Hebrew, as we have seen, prefers the verb "to say", "to declare" or "to speak" (דָּבָר or קָרָא, אָמַר) to the Greek's noun "Word", (ὁ λόγος). Thus we find in Genesis, In the beginning[241] God said, "Let there be light"; and there was light.[242] God called (named) the light Day, and the darkness he called (named) Night.[243]

To pursue this idea one step further, all speaking is in fact, so far as the Bible is concerned, calling out the names of things or "naming". Thus, to name something is to give it its reality. In Genesis we hear in the first verses that "God said 'Let there be Light' and there was light." God named the thing before he created it; the naming seems a necessary first step toward creation. The same idea is at work in the Book of Sirach (Ecclesiasticus):

> Next, I shall remind you of the works of the Lord, and tell of what I have seen. By the words (by the speaking) of the Lord his works come into being and all creation obeys (manifests) his will. (באומר אלהים רצונו ופועל רצונו לקחו)[244]

Then, according to Genesis, God gave Man the right to name all the animals and, at the same time, the right of dominion over them:

> So out of the ground the LORD God formed every animal of the field and every bird of the air, and brought them to the man to see what he would call them; and whatever the man called every living creature, that was its name. The man gave names to all cattle, and to the birds of the air, and to every animal of the field; but for the man there was not found a helper as his partner.[245]

---

[240] Joh 1:14 (NRS) and (BGT). Christians call this "incarnation" or "enfleshment", by which they mean "becoming reality".
[241] Gen 1:1 (NRS)
[242] Gen 1:3 (NRS)
[243] Gen 1:5 (NRS)
[244] Sir 42:15 (NJB)
[245] Gen 2:19-20 (NRS)

Here again the act of naming carries with it a sense of having authority over that which is named on the principle that if you create it, you have ownership and control over it.[246]

We know also, for example, that first mother and then parents name a baby's world into reality. If a baby's mother speaks French, the child's world will be a French world – in reality. If the baby's mother names certain feelings for the child, those feelings will also be a part of the child's world or reality. If the mother attaches the name "love" to the nurturing indulgence of the baby in its infancy, the child's reality will include that kind of love; if mother does not give the name, or, worse, fails to show it, the child's reality will be defective. Parents create the reality, the world of their child just as God created the universe by naming it into reality. This is not teaching the child about the world; it is creating the world of the child and is pre-rational. We might call this "Narrative Reality", and it is certainly an important concept in understanding the mind-set of the Bible which is quite different from our own. In the Bible, remembering or recollecting (זכר[247]) an event and speaking it out (in narrative) is to make it "fact" and "real", in any present time and place. Here is the reason that a scientific mind-set such as our own is tempted to reject the Bible as "mythology" and "unreal".

The principle arises from the gift of God to humankind of imagination, a gift most apparent and at work in children. Children's stories, fairy stories, tales and even epic the ballads and lays of bards and singers of old time are more than simple entertainment. The imagination of the hearers is able to give a reality to the tale which science would dismiss as foolishness and unreal. All spoken art forms touch the imagination of the hearers and take on reality which is substantial.[248] This is true for religion

---

[246] We remember, for example, the mysterious disease which broke out in 1976 in the USA which could not be studied for its treatment until it was named and made "real" a year later – Legionnaire's Disease.
[247] In Hebrew the meaning is both 1. "mention" and — 2. "remember".
[248] This includes drama on the radio. Television, sadly, removes the imagination and defines what the reality must be.

as well. In the Bible, we have already noted the power of the unexplained parable (as in the Parable of the Sower described above – but not the allegory of the seed). Thus I imagine the action of the parable in my imagination, and it becomes a reality for me in my own life, and my personal world is formed and informed by it.

An extension of the biblical parable is the longer form of it called "liturgy". The recitation of the biblical liturgy is often confused by moderns with "history". Its purpose, however, is not simple recall of event; rather, it actually re-creates the reality of the event narrated in the hearer's own time and place. The hearer actually experiences (and takes part in) the event spoken in the here and now.

When the people of Israel finally come into the Promised Land from the wilderness, a way must be found for them to become a real participant in the formative wilderness experience which God had prepared for them and which is, from generation to generation, the continuing source of their authentic religion. Therefore they are given a liturgy to bind them to the wilderness in Moses' final instructions to them before entering the Promised Land, as we have quoted above:

> You shall go to the priest who is in office at that time, and say to him, "Today I declare to the LORD your God that I have come into the land that the LORD swore to our ancestors to give us." When the priest takes the basket from your hand and sets it down before the altar of the LORD your God, you shall make this response before the LORD your God: "A wandering Aramean was my ancestor; he went down into Egypt and lived there as an alien, few in number, and there he became a great nation, mighty and populous. When the Egyptians treated us harshly and afflicted us, by imposing hard labor on us, we cried to the LORD, the God of our ancestors; the LORD heard our voice and saw our affliction, our toil, and our oppression. The LORD brought us out of Egypt with a mighty hand and an outstretched arm, with a terrifying display of power, and with signs and wonders; and he brought us into this place and gave us this land,

a land flowing with milk and honey. So now I bring the first of the fruit of the ground that you, O LORD, have given me." You shall set it down before the LORD your God and bow down before the LORD your God. Then you, together with the Levites and the aliens who reside among you, shall celebrate with all the bounty that the LORD your God has given to you and to your house.[249]

Note that this is an annual declaration at the time of the first grain harvested. It is most likely the earliest form of what is called today the Haggadah, or narrative, which is recited annually at the Feast of Passover and the intent of which is to associate Jews with the Egypt/Wilderness experience and to make this experience of the Wilderness a real part of their present lives. In the present-day Haggadah, especially directed at the children, who must also be brought into the reality of the Wilderness in every generation, four questions are posed (in the present tense and about the present meal) by four children, representing four types of people, wise, evil, simple, or unable even to ask the right question and beginning with the youngest child present:

What makes this night different from all [other] nights?

1) On all nights we need not dip even once, on this night we do so twice?

2) On all nights we eat chametz (leavened bread) or matzah (unleavened bread), and on this night only matzah?

3) On all nights we eat any kind of vegetables, and on this night maror (bitter herbs)?

4) On all nights we eat sitting upright or reclining, and on this night we all recline?

The "evil child" is called evil simply because he refuses to become part of the reality of the narrative. As my friend Rabbi Lawrence Hoffman[250] has stated it:

The notion of four childhood types derives from the fact that the Torah pictures our retelling the story four separate times, one of them in response to a child who says, "What is this service to you?" [Ex: 12:26], as if to say, "To you, not to me!" The Talmud Yerushalmi has the evil child add, "What is all this burden that you impose upon us year after year?" Evil children, then, are

---

[249] Deu 26:3-11 (NRS)
[250] See his, *Beyond the Text: A Holistic Approach to Liturgy*, in 1987.

those who willfully read themselves out of the chain of Jewish tradition.

This narrative reality is to be found also in the primitive Christian Haggadah of St. Paul:

> For I received from the Lord what I also handed on to you, that the Lord Jesus on the night when he was betrayed took a loaf of bread, and when he had given thanks, he broke it and said, "This is my body that is for you. Do this in remembrance of me (εἰς τὴν ἐμὴν ἀνάμνησιν)." In the same way he took the cup also, after supper, saying, "This cup is the new covenant in my blood. Do this, as often as you drink it, in remembrance of me." For as often as you eat this bread and drink the cup, you proclaim the Lord's death until he comes. Whoever, therefore, eats the bread or drinks the cup of the Lord in an unworthy manner will be answerable for the body and blood of the Lord. Examine yourselves, and only then eat of the bread and drink of the cup. For all who eat and drink without discerning the body, eat and drink judgment against themselves.[251]

The remembrance (ἀνάμνησιν, לְזִכְרִי, לדוכרני) is the re-creation of the reality of the sacrifice of the Lord, here and now. In fact, when the Catholic priest speaks the word over bread and wine, breathing a new name over them, they become here and now a new reality, the Body and Blood of Christ.

The final command of Jesus to his disciples at his Ascension is as follows: "And he said to them, 'Go into all the world and proclaim the good news to the whole creation'."[252] And in a different context, "But Jesus said to him, 'Let the dead bury their own dead; but as for you, go and proclaim the kingdom of God.'"[253] As for Jesus' command to preach/proclaim the Gospel (κηρύξατε, קְרָאוּ, אכרזו) and proclaim/announce the Kingdom (διάγγελλε, הוֹדַע, סבר), what he is really commanding his disciples is to go out and <u>create</u> the Kingdom of Heaven, here and now and in all the world. The mission is not just "telling about"; rather it is to make it a reality.

---

[251] 1Co 11:23-29 (NRS)
[252] Mar 16:15 (NRS)
[253] Luk 9:60 (NRS)

Narrative Reality is, for the Bible, a real and present reality which involves speaking the Word of God to the world, the goodness of which has been marred by human abuse.

We might wonder where such an understanding of reality arises. In all probability it arises in ancient Egypt. This is not to say that Israel simply copied something from Egypt, but that they were a part of a mind-set that shared categories of thought with Egypt. The difference is that while Egypt worked these categories into their own god-system anchored on the institution of the pharaoh, Israel attributed everything to God alone.

In very ancient Egypt, the idea that names/words become realities is attached to the stories of the god of creation and architecture, Ptah, an ancient deity of the ancient Memphis.

Thus all the gods were formed and his Ennead was completed. Indeed, all the divine order really came into being through what the heart thought and the tongue commanded. According to the young student of Egyptology, Caroline Seawright:

> Ptah was the chief god of the ancient city of Memphis. He was a creator god who brought all things to being by thinking of them with his mind and saying their names with his tongue. He was unique amongst Egyptian creation gods in that his methods were intellectual, rather than physical. According to the priests of Memphis, everything is the work of Ptah's heart and tongue *(idea and word)*[254]: gods are born, towns are founded, and order is maintained.[255]

The Egyptian god Ptah allegedly had the power to create anything he could name.

If we are to read the Bible correctly, we must allow this ancient definition of non-scientific reality. To understand that for the Bible, remembrance and recollection, proclamation and naming

---

[254] My italics
[255] http://www.thekeep.org/~kunoichi/kunoichi/themestream/ptah.html#.Uad17ECThc U#ixzz2UnB7SvXZ © Caroline Seawright

produce reality is to resolve much modern, scientific and historical criticism of the Bible's message.

Assertion 28: An item of reality which has featured in our modern world, especially since the development of psychology, is emotion and feeling. We have come to speak of feelings as important in our human world-view, attributing them sometimes even to animals. We are speaking here not of the physical feelings attendant upon instinctual responses of all animal life such as pain or thirst. Psychological feelings are the more refined ones such as anxiety and depression. While some of these feelings have words that seem to refer to them in Scripture, it is important to note that the emotional life of human beings is of little consequence in the Bible and do not describe reality in the Scriptures. Feelings are, for the Bible, transitory movements which come and go like the wind and have no substantive reality, neither motivating, directing, explaining nor excusing behavior.

Of course there are expressions of strong passion, even on God's part; but they are strong responses to events:
> the LORD will be unwilling to pardon them, for the LORD's anger and passion will smoke against them.[256]
> "Phinehas son of Eleazar, son of Aaron the priest, has turned back my wrath from the Israelites by manifesting such zeal among them on my behalf that in my jealousy I did not consume the Israelites.[257]
> Look down from heaven and see, from your holy and glorious habitation. Where are your zeal and your might? The yearning of your heart and your compassion? They are withheld from me.[258]

Where we might expect to find passion or arousal, there is none at all:
> It happened, late one afternoon, when David rose from his couch and was walking about on the roof of the king's house, that he saw from the roof a woman bathing; the woman was very beautiful. David sent someone to inquire about the woman. It

---
[256] Deu 29:20 (NRS)
[257] Num 25:11 (NRS)
[258] Isa 63:15 (NRS)

was reported, "This is Bathsheba daughter of Eliam, the wife of Uriah the Hittite." So David sent messengers to get her, and she came to him, and he lay with her.[259]

David's reaction to a beautiful naked woman in the moonlight does not require a great deal of analysis of David's or Bathsheba's feelings! In fact, we can say that the momentary heat of passion led to serious sin – the murder by David, of Uriah, Bath-Sheba's husband. Love, in the biblical sense, would never lead to sin.

In our modern age of psychology, we often speak of feelings of guilt, especially with regard to religion and before God. One might be tempted to say that in the above story of David and Bathsheba, David should have felt guilty for what he did. The Bible, however, would never entertain a notion of "feeling guilty". The biblical word for guilt is always objective and has nothing to do with feelings or emotions. "Guilt" has to do with culpability or liability, not emotions. It is often parallel to "sin" or judicial "blame" no matter how the person feels. It is possible for someone to acknowledge their guilt and perhaps feel badly about it even to the point of remorse , especially if punishment is involved. However, emotional self-punishment by feelings of guilt is a concept foreign to the Bible.[260] "Guilt offerings" are designed to alleviate culpability by offering compensation: and shall confess the sin that has been committed: "The person shall make *full restitution* for the wrong, adding one fifth to it, and giving it to the one who was wronged."[261] This is true with Christian sacramental Penance as well; it is certainly not to make God feel better, nor is the goal to make the penitent feel better. This may, of course, be a consequence but it is not the point at all!

The single word which suffers worst in translation from the Bible to our modern life because of the modern concern with feelings is the word "love". So different is the modern word from the

---

[259] 2Sa 11:2-4 (NRS)

[260] Perhaps parents in biblical times simply pointed out right and wrong without attaching emotional negative penalties or fears of eternal punishments to wrong behaviours (as in, "If you do thus and so you will go to hell").

[261] Num 5:7 (NRS)

biblical, that they are nearly two different words entirely. In modern usage, "love" signifies some level of passion and emotional intensity. It is used regarding inanimate things ("I love my new car!"), non-human animate things ("I love my dog!"), events ("I really loved the rock concert!"), humans of all sorts ("I love my new neighbours, my friends, my family, my wife or my "lover"!"). Sometimes the emotional content is only one of preference or "liking"; sometimes it is highly sexually charged. Because it is a feeling word, it often has a transitory life – here today (or at this moment anyway – and gone tomorrow (or in a few moments at best). Today I am passionately in love; tomorrow my ardour has cooled. This "love" has little durability simply because it is a feeling. Where it truly becomes troublesome is when two men or two women use their love for each other as a basis for gay marriage. And when it comes to religion, it makes it difficult for us to talk about the love of God (transitory?) or my love for God (equally transitory?). There is probably little that can be done about this admittedly sloppy use of the contemporary word, and when it becomes the foundation for life decisions and choices, it is certainly a foundation built on quicksand. We "fall in love" and get married, but then "fall out of love" and get divorced. When children are told that parents love them but the parents' love for each other is so transitory, small wonder that modern children are insecure.

The question arises, "Can we command feelings/" "Can I order someone to have a feelings?" Clearly, the answer is, "No!" Yet the Bible says, "You shall love the LORD your God with all your heart, and with all your soul, and with all your might."[262] And again it says, "You shall not take vengeance or bear a grudge against any of your people, but you shall love your neighbor as yourself: I am the LORD."[263] There is no question that these are two orders or commandments to love. And since feelings cannot be ordered or commanded, we are left with no alternative other

---

[262] Deu 6:5 (NRS)
[263] Lev 19:18 (NRS)

than understanding that "love" in the Bible is not a feeling or emotional word at all.

The confusion may arise from a serious difference in anatomy from the Bible to modern parlance. If we consider that the standard Valentine's Day card of modern times features a heart, we are accustomed to think of the heart as the seat of the emotion and feeling of love. In biblical times (and this includes the time of Jesus) the heart is also the anatomical seat and source of love. But the ancients did not believe the heart to be the home of feelings. Rather, the heart was the seat of the mind and will. We would say that the mind and will are in the brain and in the head; the ancients did not know what the brains were for at all. In ancient Egypt, when a person died, all of their organs as well as their body were carefully preserved for the afterlife. The brain, however, was first hooked through the nose and drawn out, only to be thrown away as having no purpose to the person.

What we think of as the function of the brain, the mind and the will, was attributed to the heart by the ancients. For them, the seat of the feelings was further down in the anatomy, usually the viscera or loins! Biblical love does indeed come from the heart ("You shall love the Lord your God with all your heart"), but love means your will and commitment – a conscious decision of free will – having absolutely nothing to do with feelings!

Furthermore, "love" is a technical word in the Bible. We find in Genesis 22 the order of God to Abraham: "He said, 'Take your son, your only son Isaac, <u>whom you love,</u> and go to the land of Moriah, and offer him there as a burnt offering on one of the mountains that I shall show you.'"[264]   This is not to suggest that Abraham does not love his other son Ishmael (or probably Eliezar of Damascus), but that Isaac is the son who will inherit the covenant God made first with Abraham. When Moses declares God's blessing on the People of Israel, Moses declares:

---

[264] Gen 22:2 (NRS)

> He will love you, bless you, and multiply you; he will bless the fruit of your womb and the fruit of your ground, your grain and your wine and your oil, the increase of your cattle and the issue of your flock, in the land that he swore to your ancestors to give you.[265]

The meaning of love here is the same as with Isaac. God will treat Israel as his inheriting offspring, his favourite and elect. There is no emotion involved. When Joshua later instructs the people about life in the Promised Land, he directs them:

> Take good care to observe the commandment and instruction that Moses the servant of the LORD commanded you, to love the LORD your God, to walk in all his ways, to keep his commandments, and to hold fast to him, and to serve him with all your heart and with all your soul[266]

He is clearly addressing their will for the future and not their feelings at the present moment.

We find the very disturbing passage at the beginning of the Book of the Prophet Malachi:

> I have loved you, says the LORD. But you say, "How have you loved us?" Is not Esau Jacob's brother? says the LORD. Yet I have loved Jacob but I have hated Esau;[267]

Can it be that God hates? Can it be that God plays favourites between Jacob and Esau (the People of Israel and the People of Edom)? Such a mistranslation of "love" and "hate" have led to all kinds of spurious and hateful theological developments, especially in Christian thinking. We have only to recall that the specious doctrines of predestination – to salvation and to damnation – have arisen from attributing vicious "hatred" to God.[268]

---

[265] Deu 7:13 (NRS)
[266] Jos 22:5 (NRS)
[267] Mal 1:2-3 (NRS)
[268] Thankfully this tendency has been countered by such declarations as we find in the Anglican Prayer Book's collect for Ash Wednesday: "Almighty and everlasting God, who hatest nothing that thou has made, and dost forgive the sins of all those who are penitent: Create and make in us new and contrite hearts, that we, worthily lamenting our sins and acknowledging our wretchedness, may obtain of thee, the God of all mercy, perfect remission and forgiveness; through Jesus Christ our Lord. Amen."

The simple solution is a proper understanding of "love" and "hate" in the Bible as dispassionate words. In the case of Malachi before us, the appropriate translation is: "I have favoured you, says the LORD. But you say, 'How have you favoured us?' Is not Esau Jacob's brother? says the LORD. Yet I have favoured Jacob over Esau." When the Bible uses "love" and "hate" together, the translation is "to prefer (love) one over the other (hate). There is nothing to do with passion or emotion, much less viciousness. It is the biblical way of expressing preference.

In addition to the technical meanings of the word "love", we also find the word used in a basic and physical sense. When Samson first met Delilah, the Bible says: "After this he fell in love with a woman in the valley of Sorek, whose name was Delilah."[269] This sounds like a use of the word ("fell in love with") in an emotional sense. But a better translation is found in the Revised Standard Version, "After this he loved a woman in the valley of Sorek, whose name was Delilah."[270] The Hebrew makes it clear that Samson had sex with Delilah in the valley of Sorek (and made an alliance with her, i.e. she became his mistress). There is no passionate love affair with Delilah described here (though indeed their relationship may very well have been passionate, though it is hardly the point of the story of Samson and Delilah).

Much has been made of the love of Jonathan and David. "Jonathan made David swear again by his love for him; for he loved him as he loved his own life."[271] A modern interpretation based upon the passion and sexual passion of "love" has interpreted this relationship as a homosexual one. David's lament over the dead Jonathan seems to add fuel to this fire: "I am distressed for you, my brother Jonathan; greatly beloved were you to me; your love to me was wonderful, passing the love of women."[272]

---

[269] Jdg 16:4 (NRS)
[270] Jdg 16:4 (RSV)
[271] 1Sa 20:17 (NRS)
[272] 2Sa 1:26 (NRS)

If, however, we read this passage with the non-passionate definition of "love" which is the Bible's, we must consider other, more important qualities such as commitment and fidelity. Jonathan is the crown prince, son of King Saul and next in line to be king of Israel – by birth. David is, on the other hand, a commoner and a warlord with no regal claims at all. Yet David and Jonathan are committed to each other in a way that is closer even than a marital covenant/contract.[273]

Jonathan knows that God has taken the kingdom away from his father Saul and given it to David. There is no jealousy about this, only faithful love. Jonathan is willing to give his patrimony to David in the future, for that is what God wants. All he asks is that his own crippled son might be protected by David so that he, Jonathan, would have progeny in the future:

> Saul's son Jonathan had a son who was crippled in his feet. He was five years old when the news about Saul and Jonathan came from Jezreel. His nurse picked him up and fled; and, in her haste to flee, it happened that he fell and became lame. His name was Mephibosheth.[274]

Such a commitment on David's part concerning Jonathan's son is also dangerous for David, for Mephibosheth might well claim the kingdom back from David – who is, after all, a usurper. David's promise arises out of his love for Jonathan, even though it is not politic. Thus we read: "But the king spared Mephibosheth, the son of Saul's son Jonathan, because of the oath of the LORD that

---

[273] We must note that both men have wives and children – sexuality is not the issue here; only the kingdom. The relationship of Alexander the Great and his friend from childhood, Hephaistion, might approximate the relationship between David and Jonathan, if we ignore the rumours of a homosexual alliance between the two Macedonians, for they are only rumours and irrelevant to the real issue. Alexander says that Hephaistion is his alter ego – "we are both Alexander" he says to the Persian Queen. They share secrets with each other – they are of one mind. This is more than simple intimacy – it is a faithful commitment, wanting the best for each other as for the self. This same kind of love which touches upon the very life and death of the principles is to be seen in the relationship between Ruth and her mother-in-law Naomi: " Where you go, I will go; where you lodge, I will lodge; your people shall be my people, and your God my God. Where you die, I will die-- there will I be buried. May the LORD do thus and so to me, and more as well, if even death parts me from you!" Rut 1:16-17 (NRS).
[274] 2Sa 4:4 (NRS)

was between them, between David and Jonathan son of Saul."[275] This was at a time when Mephibosheth might well have claimed the kingdom back for himself and the family of Saul, his grandfather. In short, Jonathan gave his life and his kingdom for David out of love. There is no feeling or emotional content involved in this; it is a phenomenal and sacrificial force of will and fidelity. And it is grounded in the will of God.

This story of David and Jonathan is perhaps behind the Gospel of John's description of the relationship between Jesus, the son of David, and the disciple John ("one of his disciples-- the one whom Jesus loved")[276]. On the cross, Jesus, the son of David gives the kingdom back to the "son" of Jonathan with the same selfless, faithful and sacrificial love as was there in the first narrative:

> When Jesus saw his mother and the disciple whom he loved standing beside her, he said to his mother, "Woman, here is your son." Then he said to the disciple, "Here is your mother." And from that hour the disciple took her into his own home.[277]

This kind of love (Hebrew, אָהַב) is also called "faithful or enduring love" (Hebrew, חֶסֶד). Again this is love based upon conviction, commitment and steadfastness of will. It is connected to loyalty, upon faithfulness and upon a firmness of resolve for the future. There is nothing of the transitoriness of feeling associated with it. It is very often used to describe God's relationship with Israel, particularly in the Psalms. The purpose of the will attached to love in the Bible often has covenantal and contractual implications which take no notice of emotion or feelings.

Assertion 29: Scripture is not history or even historical. It would be folly to attempt the dating of events or narratives to be found in the Bible. However, the Bible, especially the Old Testament, is self-consciously epochal and rather generally divided into epochs or eras which are connected to form a whole narrative,

---

[275] 2Sa 21:7 (NRS)
[276] Joh 13:23 (NRS)
[277] Joh 19:26-27 (NRS)

from the beginning to the close of the biblical period. These eras are vaguely called "the generations" (Hebrew תוֹלְדוֹת), as in the summary of the first era: "These are the generations of the heavens and the earth when they were created."[278] No date for this is even implied, but it does tell us that this is first epoch of the world-story. It comes, of course, at the beginning of the story. The Greek equivalent is γενεάς: "Remember the deeds of the ancestors, which they did in their generations; and you will receive great honor and an everlasting name."[279] No era is meant to be dated in any historical sense; however, the eras have an order, one happening before another, and the third happening after the second. Perhaps a less formal definition would be "at the time of …", as: "Now it came to pass, *in the days when* (בִּימֵי [280]) the judges ruled, that there was a famine in the land."[281]

The present Hebrew Bible follows a very general sense of these eras, having three distinct but connected parts: the Torah, the Prophets and the Writings. The Torah comes first.[282] There follows the "book" of the prophets, and this division includes the books which cover generally the time from the entrance of the Israelites into the Land of Israel until the Babylonian captivity of Judah (the "days of prophecy")[283]. Finally come the Writings, which include all the rest of the biblical books, mostly attributed to the days of the Babylonian Exile (though the Book of Ruth is included here).

---

[278] Gen 2:4 (NRS)
[279] 1Ma 2:51 (NRS)
[280] Rut 1:1 (WTT)
[281] Rut 1:1 (NKJ)
[282] These are the five books attributed to Moses: Genesis, Exodus, Leviticus, Numbers and Deuteronomy.
[283] These days include everything from the crossing of the Jordan (Joshua, Judges) to the end of the Kingdom of Judah – though the Exilic prophets Haggai, Zechariah and Malachi are also included.

Since this organizational method according to eras is arbitrary and artificial, for the purposes of this work I would propose the following arbitrary structure:

Prelude: The Bible begins with what it calls the "Generations of the Heavens and the Earth, by which it means the story of the creation by God of the world. It is straightforward and includes the narrative of the creation of humankind.

Beginnings of Humankind: These are the days of humankind's spreading throughout the earth and include the stories of long-ago giants, long-lived heroes and various righteous men. It is the time of Noah and the Generation of the Tower of Babel. There are lessons to be learned here about humankind generally, though they are not history lessons. We might think of it as the first days of the Gentiles, for there was no Israel or Judaism. This section represents the spreading of the sin of Cain (i.e. murder and the offenses against life) throughout the world and God's increasing frustration with humankind about sin. It establishes the basic "problem" of the world and the continuing attempts of God to deal with the problem. It is to this period that Israel, after the Babylonian Exile, will look to make sense of the destruction of its national life and Israel's finding themselves amongst the nations once again. Hidden in this era are the seeds of mission – God's mission to recall the world and humankind (the Gentiles) to himself. It is to this mission of God that his people will slowly return following the collapse of their national experiment.

The Time of the Patriarchs: God's method of making himself known in a world alienated from the Creator is to begin small, with one man and his family. Abraham is a Gentile, and the only thing that differentiates him from any other Gentile of his world is his willingness and choice to accept the God who comes to him unexpectedly in Genesis 12 and to act on and invitation to come apart from the Gentile world and to become a people who belong to this God. The promises of this God are really no different from the promise of many other deities, namely long life (through many generations) and the opportunity to share in the land belonging to this God and its wealth. Abraham is to enjoy the protection of this particular God rather than the gods of the nations whose protection and wealth he enjoyed previously in Ur. Abraham's singularity is due to the singularity of this God he has chosen and not to anything special about Abraham. The real point to this exchange between God and Abraham is God's decision to re-introduce himself to the world through the system humankind has developed for itself of having national gods. Clearly, God involves himself in human lives through the institutions that human develop for themselves.

The central point of this period is the mutual exploration of the land which will become the Promised Land and a time of "getting to know you" on the part of each. The Patriarchs, and especially Abraham, go from place to place, setting up altars and sacred stones and then "call on God's Name" at those places. It is as though by doing this, the patriarch lays claim to the land in the name of and on God's behalf. It is rather like Columbus, discovering a new land, planting the flag of Spain, and calling out the name of the King/Queen of Spain as the new owners. The patriarch explores the land on his own and God's behalf, roving up and down the land.

At the end of the patriarch narrative, in the Joseph story, it is shown how the people of Israel move from the land of promise down into Egypt by reason of famine. They lose their identity as the people of God in Egypt and, because they are outside the Promised Land, have no communication with God.

The Days of the Exodus and the Years of the Wilderness: These are the events from the birth of Moses to the crossing of the Jordan River. For the Bible, and this includes the New Testament, this is the era of the birth and early life of Israel. The institutions developed in this time become normative for the People of God and their self-understanding and their purpose. There are scholars who would claim that in fact the peoples of this time are quite primitive and unsophisticated both in culture and in religion. They perceive that they could only be a non-descript motely, runaway slaves from Egypt wandering like Bedouin in the desert. These same scholars would claim that the real sophistication of Israel's religion was developed during the Babylonian exile and then read back into this period to give it authenticity. The principle here seems to be that the later in time a civilisation, the less primitive it will be. This is, of course, rubbish; nothing could be further from the truth.

The truth is that the first people of Israel came from the most sophisticated and advanced culture of the world of that time. And while they rejected the gods and religion of Egypt, they also left with all of the abilities and cultural treasures of that nation. This is perhaps signified by God's command that they leave with the treasure of their neighbours: "The Israelites had done as Moses told them; they had asked the Egyptians for jewellery of silver and gold, and for clothing," [284] Two primary Egyptian deities, Thoth and his consort, Ma'at, represent two cultural sophistications which are not rejected by Israel. Thoth is wisdom in the sense of the wisdom of creation itself – the calculations which design and maintain creation. This is very similar to the Greek concept of "the Word" (ὁ λόγος)[285] and of God's speaking the Word of creation (καὶ εἶπεν ὁ θεός).[286] Thoth is also the Scribe of the gods and the master of the written word. Egypt has, of course, a most advanced literary tradition. Further, Thoth is the master of both the physical laws but also the moral laws which govern society. He maintains the balance of things, including good and evil, in creation. Far from rejecting all of this, the people of Israel simply attributed it all to the Lord God of Israel.

The same is true of Thoth's consort, Ma'at, whose functions are frequently the same as those of Thoth, namely justice and righteousness, the social order and balance, and judicial and moral

---

[284] Exo 12:35 (NRS)
[285] Joh 1:1 (BGT)
[286] Gen 1:3 (BGT)

truth, (Hebr., הָאֱמֶת).[287]   She is signified by the feather against which the souls of the departed would be weighed for entrance to immortality. Both Thoth and his sister/wife were under the jurisdiction of the Egyptian creator-God Ra and were shown together riding in the boat of Ra (the sun).[288]

The point of all this is not particularly to show absolute parallels between Israel's religion and that of Egypt, but to show that the people coming out of Egypt in the Exodus were not the hapless and ignorant "slaves" without cultural sophistication or ability as is sometimes portrayed of them. There is absolutely no reason to think that the development of Israel's religion had to await the Babylonian Exile or that it was read back onto the time of the Exodus from much later. A single example will suffice. We find written in the Book of Deuteronomy: "That very day Moses wrote this song (ode) and taught it to the Israelites."[289]   There is no reason to suppose that he did not write it or that it was attributed to Moses from a later time.

I will have more to say below about the institution of the Levites arising in the time of the Wilderness. They are most certainly the tribe of Israel most concerned with scribal and legal matters. They are the Tribe of Moses, his brother Aaron, the High Priest and his sister, Miriam the Prophetess. Moses and his family, while Israelites, were clearly highly placed in the royal family, court and temple society of Egypt. Even if there are some illiterates coming out of Egypt in the Exodus, there were many who were not. Just as Abraham came out of Ur of the Chaldeans a rich, powerful and learned man who converted from the complex god-system of his city to the simplicity of the One God, so the people of Israel came out of Egypt with a cultural and monetary wealth, again convinced of the power of the One God and forsaking only the Egyptian gods.

---

[287] Gen 42:16 (WTT)
[288] Perhaps this Egyptian "Trinity" of Creator (Ra), Word (Thoth) and Spirit of Truth (Ma'at) come to the Christian Church through the creation stories of Genesis, which seem to be Israel's recasting of its Egyptian heritage.
[289] Deu 31:22 (NRS)

It is most likely that the narratives of the Exodus and the Wilderness are real-time reports and not imaginary stories from a later time and distant place.

The Time of the Conquest and the Judges: This period, from the crossing of the Jordan River to the time of the Prophet Samuel represents a continuation of the Wilderness Period into the occupation of the Promised Land. It is the time in which Israel attempts, more or less successfully, to implement the lessons of the wilderness in the place of permanent settlement. The crisis of this time is whether to continue the faith-based and very fluid traditions of the wilderness or to assimilate the traditions of the people of the land – a people of cities and towns and multiple deities, an agricultural and settled society which have enjoyed success in economics and warfare. The period ends in the almost total "eclipse" of the Wilderness Tradition with the establishment of the "Empire" of King Solomon.

The Times of the Kingdoms, the Babylonian Exile; the Restoration; and the Destruction of the Temple by Rome: The corruption of the later kings (and probably also the High Priesthood) led to the weakness of the state and its vulnerability to its neighbours, especially the Babylonians, who, under King Nebuchadnezzar, destroyed the city and the Temple in 587/586 BCE. The leadership of the Judaean community was taken into exile in Babylon and established a Judaean community there, which ultimately became one of the largest and most important in the world. However, having no Temple and priestly establishment to occupy them, a new definition of the People of God began to emerge there. There is no indication, however, that the Jerusalem feasts – Passover/Shavuot and Sukkot were celebrated there. There was neither altar nor priesthood for the celebrations.

With the Persian overthrow of Babylon, a new policy towards conquered lands emerged, namely to seek support for the Persian king from all the gods of conquered peoples. Under this regime, a group of Judaeans (Zerubbabel, Ezra, etc.) were urged to return to Jerusalem and, without a king, rebuild the Temple and the city:

> The heads of the families of Judah and Benjamin, and the priests and the Levites-- everyone whose spirit God had stirred-- got ready to go up and rebuild the house of the LORD in Jerusalem.[290]

Note that these people were noble families of Judah and the Temple Tribe of Benjamin and the staff of the old Temple – no Israelites. The first feast they celebrated was, of course, Sukkot:

> When the seventh month came, and the Israelites were in the towns, the people gathered together in Jerusalem. Then Jeshua son of Jozadak, with his fellow priests, and Zerubbabel son of Shealtiel with his kin set out to build the altar of the God of Israel, to offer burnt offerings on it, as prescribed in the law of Moses the man of God. They set up the altar on its foundation, because they were in dread of the neighboring peoples, and they offered burnt offerings upon it to the LORD, morning and evening. And they kept the festival of booths, as prescribed, and offered the daily burnt offerings by number according to the ordinance, as required for each day, and after that the regular burnt offerings, the offerings at the new moon and at all the sacred festivals of the LORD, and the offerings of everyone who made a freewill offering to the LORD.[291]

For the most part, this was a return to status quo qui ante bellum, except with a Persian satrap in charge rather than the Davidic Messianic king. This was a Judaean establishment. If there was any local authority, it was the limited authority of the reigning High Priest (Zadokite, not Aaronic).

It must be remembered that with the Jewish people scattered over the known world in the Galuth (the Dispersion), the people and institutions of Jerusalem were a small (though powerful) minority of the Jewish community.

We can now make the following summary of the cult of Jerusalem:

---

[290] Ezr 1:5 (NRS)
[291] Ezr 3:1-5 (NRS)w

1. From Solomon onwards, Jerusalem and its Temple represented a serious centralisation of political power on the Egyptian model. The King was in a real way the representation of God himself and the palace and the temple were both called the "hêkal".
2. The religious cult was separated from the entire tradition of the Wilderness people and the prophets – the high priesthood was Solomon's local appointment, the prophets were "cult" prophets and Solomon took a central part in Temple worship.
3. A local festival of Jerusalem, with strong fertility and rain-making (as in Egypt) aspects (the water-drawing and the lulavim), solar cultism (the etrogim and the very solar observatory nature of the Temple building itself and controlled by the priests (another Egyptian likeness), from time to time, an out and out playing with magic , and a Solomonic cult of anointed kingship which centred on his father David and the covenant which was made with David (another Egyptianism) which became a cult of Davidic Messianism were all features of the cult of Jerusalem/Judah.
4. The outright rejection of the traditions of Israel (the Wilderness tradition) was accompanied by an attempt to take the cultic institutions of Israel and incorporate them into the Temple worship. This caused the ark to be brought to the Holy of Holies and the pilgrim feasts of Israel were incorporated into the sacrificial schedule of Jerusalem. The High Priesthood was removed from the promise made by God to the House of Aaron and strengthened to the point that when there was no king, the foreign Zadokite High Priest became the ruler.
5. All of the above notations about Judah/Jerusalem became so powerful, that in the later period of the Kingdom of Judah, the whole of the Temple cult became out and out pagan from time to time. The withdrawal of the northern ten tribes from Jerusalem and its cult immediately after the death of Solomon led, not to the return to the old Wilderness tradition, but the establishment of a pale copy of the Judaean cult which led to a problem worse than what existed in Judah and soon disappeared.
6. The people of Jerusalem were called Judaeans, not Israelites and certainly not Jews. In the days of the Second Temple (and King

Herod) these Judaeans, in the face of foreign occupation, became what we might call Zionists, which group had, from time to time, lunatic fringes of messianism and terrorism (the Sicarii, the Zealots, etc.). The religion was secularized and radicalized. When the Christian Gospels speak of the Jews who participated in the crucifixion of Jesus, the Greek calls them Ἰουδαίων, "Judaeans", a political party, and not anything to do with anything that we know today as Jews.

7. Jerusalem at the time of Herod was as great a cultural mess as we might note in today's Syria. It was culturally eclectic, more political than religious and above all, violent. The Roman view of it as THE problem in the empire was undoubtedly correct. In the First revolt, the Temple became what it always was meant to be – the Fortress of Jerusalem. This is why Titus destroyed it and after the attempt of Simon bar Kochba to revive the whole thing, led the Romans to sow the whole land with salt to make it uninhabitable – and to build Aelia Capitolina in its place.

Finally, we come to Rabbi Jochanan ben Zakkai and the fall of the Temple. At what became clearly the last days of the Temple, ben Zakkai was smuggled out of the fortress in a coffin. He proceeded to Javne where he established and new Judaism under the control of the Great Sanhedrin and the Rabbis that came there. Their great work was to re-form Judaism in a book (the Mishnah) and to place the governance of the people under the authority of the Sanhedrin which they established.

Their first task was to remember lovingly the institutions of the Temple and Jerusalem, and then to make sure that the Temple, its priesthood, its Davidic political messianism and its flagrant excesses WOULD NEVER BE BUILT OR RESTORED AGAIN! These Rabbis decentralized the religion by making its feasts into celebrations of the home and synagogue, which could be celebrated anywhere. Rather than priests, the fathers of families became the leaders of the celebrations. The power of the priests (cohenim) was so reduced as to become virtually non-existent. Messianism was suppressed and re-attached to the figure of Elijah.

The notion of the ideal Jerusalem was reduced to a single line in the Passover Haggadah – "Next year (not defined) in Jerusalem". Passover became the central feast but became a local table festival which centred on narrative rather than symbols. The narrative was placed in the present tense, so that all who joined the narrative became a part of it. The setting of the table varied by household but had no inherent symbolism that was crucial to it. Elijah (an Israelite prophet) joined the table as an unseen guest, but only as one who – in the vague final days – would answer all unsolved problems. Sukkoth became a feast of the home, and the sukkah, while retaining some of the harvest features, became a place where the family ate – al fresco – and attached to the home. The lulav and the etrog with their psalms were far removed from rainmaking in Jerusalem (since the time of rain in Iowa has no connection with the former rains of Jerusalem). Shavuot was disconnected from the agricultural end of the harvest (wheat and barley) in Israel and was made into a celebration of the giving of the Torah on Mt. Sinai – a feast to be kept locally in the home or the synagogue.

The Sanhedrin also made a complete disconnect of the calendar from the solar year controlled (at the equinoctial sunrise on Sukkoth, with the Temple as the observatory) by the priests. The power of the priests and the excesses of a solar cult were completely suppressed. The rabbis ordained a lunar calendar which had to be determined monthly by witnesses from the court agreeing on a new moon. Thus the court controlled the calendar. In fact, Israel was conceived again on the model of the Wilderness Tradition, but set in the context of the home and the local synagogue. All of this made it possible to be a Jew (and this was a universal designation) no matter in what area of the world one lived. It was a brilliant move and saved Judaism!